THE HEBREW POWER OF THE
PRIESTLY BLESSING UNLEASHED

Hilkiah Press

The cover of this book features the keystone of an arch inscribed with the Tetragrammaton. This unusual architectural feature appears in St. Paul's Chapel adjacent to Ground Zero in Manhattan. This *Christian* chapel with the *Hebrew* name of God survived the carnage of 9/11 without damage.

Cover design by Jürgen Heiss & S. Kim Glassman.

ISBN 978-0-9830981-2-6

http://www.HilkiahPress.com

http://www.NehemiasWall.com

Table of Contents

In loving memory of my father

RABBI ROBERT DAVID GORDON

(1941–2011)

The Priestly Blessing

(Birkat Kohanim)

May Yehovah bless you and protect you.

May Yehovah shine His face towards you and be gracious to you.

May Yehovah lift His face towards you and give you peace.

יְבָרֶכְךָ יְהֹוָה וְיִשְׁמְרֶךָ׃

יָאֵר יְהֹוָה ׀ פָּנָיו אֵלֶיךָ וִיחֻנֶּךָּ׃

יִשָּׂא יְהֹוָה ׀ פָּנָיו אֵלֶיךָ וְיָשֵׂם לְךָ שָׁלוֹם׃

Ye-va-re-che-*cha* Ye-ho-*vah* Ve-Yish-me-*re*-cha

Ya-*er* Ye-ho-*vah* Pa-*nav* E-*le*-cha Vi-chu-*ne*-ka

Yi-*sa* Ye-ho-*vah* Pa-*nav* E-*le*-cha Ve-Ya-*sem* Le-*cha* Sha-*lom*

Chapter 1:

The Thin Silent Voice

The sun rose over the mountains, revealing a line of glowing red cliffs. I was at the top of Mount Sinai with hundreds of pilgrims from all over the world, but all I could think about was the woman who broke my heart two months earlier. She dropped the news on me a few days before I was scheduled to fly out to the United States for a two-month speaking tour. It felt like she pushed her fist through my rib cage and ripped my still-beating heart out of my chest. In a daze, I traveled through the great American West. I remember driving through the forests of Colorado on my way to a speaking venue. I was in one of the most beautiful places I had ever seen but felt so emotionally numb, I was unable to enjoy it. The low point came one night in some cheap motel as I stared up at the ceiling; I lay there paralyzed with pain, minutes before I needed to go out and speak to hundreds of people. Right at the last moment, God somehow gave me the strength to get hold of myself and do what I needed to do. I don't think anyone in the audience knew what I was going through, but as soon as I got back to my room, the agony returned.

Throughout that time in the United States, I had a deep sense that I needed to get out into the desert. I wanted to erase the memory of what happened the way Jim Carrey did in the movie *Eternal Sunshine of the Spotless Mind.* After a painful breakup, Carrey underwent a futuristic procedure to have his memory purged. I knew that was science fiction but hoped the desert would somehow leave me with a "spotless mind," free of my own painful memories.[1]

---

[1] *Eternal Sunshine of the Spotless Mind*, directed by Michel Gondry, 2004.

When I arrived back in Israel, I called up a friend and we took the bus down to Eilat. From there we crossed the border into Egypt and headed south to the Bedouin village of Nuweiba. I chose Nuweiba as the spot of my desert isolation because this is where the Israelites crossed the Red Sea. I was ready to have a personal Exodus from pain at the very spot where my ancestors crossed over into freedom.

In Nuweiba, we slept in a straw hut on the coast of the Red Sea. We spent our days sprawled out on Bedouin couches on the beach, comforted by the sound of the waves lapping up on the shore only a few feet away. It was very relaxing but did nothing to lessen the immense emotional pain I was feeling. During that time on the beach, I sat there in the early morning hours and read my Bible. I read about the Israelites leaving Egypt in haste and fleeing through the desert. I read about God splitting the Red Sea and the Israelites walking across on dry land, leaving the house of bondage forever. I am always moved by reading these stories but in Nuweiba, they had a special power.

As I read the Biblical account of the Exodus, I looked back over my right shoulder at *Pi-hahiroth*, the "Mouth of the Gorges," where the newly freed slaves rushed forth onto the sandy plain of Nuweiba. There the Israelites found themselves trapped between the Red Sea and the Egyptian army. Across the sea, they could see the Land of Midian, where Moses was shepherding the flock of his father-in-law when God spoke to him from the burning bush.

I had this yearning to go to Mount Sinai but realized this was impossible. Years earlier, I learned that the real Mount Sinai was in Saudi Arabia in a region known until this very day as "Midian." I knew the Saudis would never let me visit the holy mountain. Then it occurred to me that although I could not visit the *real* Mount Sinai I might as well visit the *traditional* one. After all, God is everywhere and capable of touching our lives wherever we are.

Mount Sinai is known best as the place where God spoke the Ten Commandments to the entire nation of Israel. My desire to visit Mount Sinai had to do with something else that happened there to the prophet Elijah. The event took place during the reign of Ahab, a wicked king of Israel who married a Sidonian princess named Jezebel. Throughout the history of Israel, idolatry had always been a nagging problem but Jezebel took this to a completely new level. She was zealous for her Canaanite deities and used her power to persecute and kill the prophets of the one true God. Elijah alone stood up against Jezebel's persecutions. After his famous showdown with the prophets of Baal on Mount Carmel, Elijah fled to Mount Sinai to escape Jezebel's vengeance and to seek guidance from God. I don't have a fraction of Elijah's faith or faithfulness, but I felt like I needed to escape from the *spirit* of Jezebel and seek guidance.

I discussed the idea of visiting the mountain with my friend and then went to inquire of the Bedouin man who ran the beach encampment where we were staying. It was late in the morning, approaching noon, and the Bedouin was just waking up after a long night of smoking hashish. He rubbed his eyes and told me it would only be possible to go to Mount Sinai if we could find two more people to join us; it was a long drive and the taxi driver would only go with a minimum of four people. I headed back to the beach disappointed, but I knew that if I were meant to go to the mountain, it would happen.

A couple of hours later, the Bedouin was fully awake and walked over to the shore where we were sitting. He told us that two women had just arrived from Thailand and that they wanted to go to Mount Sinai. He said we should pack warm clothes and get some rest, because the driver would be there late that night to pick us up. It was too hot to climb the mountain during the day so the main activity there was in the middle of the night. I tried to sleep that afternoon but was too excited about my impending pilgrimage to the traditional site of Mount Sinai.

The taxi arrived at about 10 p.m., and we loaded in with the two Thai women. After a long drive, we finally arrived at the mountain about midnight. The driver told us to be back at the taxi by 9 a.m. the next morning. At the base of the mountain, we hired a Bedouin guide to take us up to the peak.

The hike up the mountain was difficult. As we walked up the old dirt trail in the dark, I kept tripping on awkward stone steps that would crop up unexpectedly. Our guide had a broken flashlight that kept blacking out. One minute we would be walking in the light; the next we would be stumbling around in the dark. The stars were brighter than I had ever seen, so I asked the Bedouin guide to turn off the flashlight. His English was not good enough to understand me, so I was stuck with the intermittent blackouts. I ended up jamming my foot against a step. At the time, I didn't realize the damage, but it would take six months for my foot to fully heal.

After about three hours of hiking in the dark, the journey was over. We reached a large stone Bedouin shelter built into the side of the mountain, about one hundred feet below the peak. With broken English and hand signals, our guide suggested that we rest in the cave-like shelter for a few hours before climbing the last section.

My friend and I sat on a mat on the floor of the candle-lit shelter, and I pulled my Bible out of my backpack. I flipped to the Book of Kings and began to read the story of Elijah's journey to Mount Sinai in Hebrew, translating into English for my friend as I read. Elijah walked for forty days and forty nights before reaching Mount Sinai. When he arrived at the top of the mountain, he lay down in a small cave and prayed for guidance. As he lay there, he heard "a great strong wind, splitting mountains and shattering rocks," but God was not in the wind.[1] Then there was an earthquake, but God was not in the earthquake. Then a fire, but God was not in the fire. Finally, Elijah heard "a still small voice" and God spoke to him through this voice.[2]

As I was reading this and translating into English, I became fascinated with the phrase "a still small voice." In Hebrew, it actually said *kol d'mamah dakah,* literally "a thin silent voice."[3] How could a voice be "silent?" And what did it really mean that the voice was "thin?" We spent some time discussing Elijah's experience on Mount Sinai and then decided that rather than waiting in the shelter, we would head for the peak.

---

[1] 1 Kings 19:11.

[2] 1 Kings 19:12 [KJV].

[3] 1 Kings 19:12.

It took less than ten minutes to reach the top of the mountain. There were hundreds of people up there from every race and dozens of nationalities. I heard many languages I recognized but more that I did not. Many of the pilgrims at the peak were shaking violently from the chilly wind. They assumed it would be as hot on the peak as it was at the foot of the mountain, and some wore nothing more than shorts and t-shirts. Thankfully, the Bedouin came to the rescue, renting out woolen blankets to the freezing visitors. We were warned to bring warm clothes so I was comfortably wrapped in several layers of shirts topped off with a hoodie.

Most of the people at the peak were concentrated around two buildings: an old church and an old mosque. I needed to get away from the wall of noise the people created, so I walked down a flight of old stone steps that led to a ruined building below the church. I sat down behind an old column, pulled my hood over my head, and began to pray. I don't think I've ever prayed so hard in my life. I came to the mountain because my heart ached and even after two months, the pain had not diminished. I sat behind that pillar and had a conversation with God, asking Him to take away the hurt.

I must have been down there for an hour when people started spilling down the steps into the ruined building where I was praying. As more and more pilgrims arrived, they were running out of room at the top. I decided to get up and look for my friend. I pushed through the throng of people, bounding up the steps towards the highest part of the peak. At a certain point, I could not go any further. I decided to lay claim to a small patch of ground about midway between the church and the mosque. My plan was to wait there until sunrise, which, by now, was less than an hour away.

I stood there staring at the horizon as the pre-dawn light turned the sky a deep blue. There was a group of Africans I assumed to be Kenyans behind me. Every now and then they would break out into the most beautiful *a cappella* singing. I had no idea what they were singing about, but I imagined it was some sort of religious music. I decided to pull my hood over my head and to go back to praying. I didn't want to nag God, but the pain in my heart hadn't subsided. As I prayed and the Kenyans sang, I suddenly recognized one word in their music. It was a Hebrew word, or rather, two Hebrew words, which often are joined together in the Bible as *Hallelujah*, "Praise Yah." They were praising God using the poetic form of His name that appears dozens of times in the Hebrew Bible.[1] I couldn't believe it. I was on a mountaintop in the middle of the desert, and these people I didn't know, speaking a language I couldn't understand, were praising the name of the one true God in perfect Hebrew. I had no idea what the rest of the song was about, but they kept coming back to "Hallelujah" in the chorus. By this time, the first rays of the sun started to shine forth over the horizon, turning the mountains that surround Mount Sinai a beautiful reddish-brown.

As the Kenyans praised the name of Yah one more time, something happened to me, something I never experienced before. A wave of emotion suddenly overcame me and, out of nowhere, I burst into tears. I don't know if it lasted ten minutes or ten seconds. Time seemed to stand still. I suddenly felt God's love in a way I've never felt it before. Not just in some intellectual way of knowing that God loves me, but in a very real and tangible way. In my mind's eye, I could see God looking down from heaven at me and hear Him say, "I'm going to take the pain off your shoulders and carry it for you." I then felt the hand of Yah reach down and take my pain away.

From that moment, the numbing pain was gone. I'm not saying it didn't still hurt, but the feelings of emptiness and despair were gone. For two months, I had been looking out at the world through a veil of sadness, overwhelmed by hopelessness. Then I heard the *thin silent voice* and that all evaporated in an instant. I didn't have a *spotless mind* like Jim Carrey in that movie, but I felt like a human being again, invigorated by the morning chill. I suddenly noticed that my foot was aching where I smashed it on the step on the way up the mountain. I joyfully embraced the pain because it meant I could feel again.

---

[1] *Yah*, the poetic form of God's name, first appears in the *Song of the Sea* (Exodus 15:2). It occurs a total of forty-nine times in the Hebrew Bible, including twenty-four as part of "Hallelujah." It also appears in the New Testament four times as part of "Hallelujah" (Revelation 19:1, 3–4, 6).

After sunrise, there was a rush of pilgrims heading down from the peak. A bottleneck of human traffic formed at the top of the narrow steps leading to the Bedouin shelter. As I slowly made my way through the swarm of people, I gave a great deal of thought to what had happened. Intellectually I knew I had gone through what secular scholars call a "mystical experience." As a Jew whose ancestors were exiled for more than a thousand years in Lithuania, my automatic reflex was to reject the validity of my own experience.

Before the Holocaust, the Jews of Lithuania—known as *Litvaks*—were considered the intellectual elite of the Jewish world. This was a well-deserved reputation earned through centuries of book learning and study. Part of my upbringing as a Litvak Jew was to distrust anything deemed "too spiritual." I was always taught to dismiss dreams, miracles, and mystical experiences as folk superstition.

I knew the Litvak explanation would be that severe exhaustion, lack of sleep, climbing a mountain in the dark, and two months of extreme emotional stress had combined to trigger this unusual experience. To be honest, if anyone else had told me this happened to him, that would definitely have been my response to it. Having experienced it myself, I was not satisfied with a mere bio-physiological explanation. Throughout my life, I have had a number of, what seemed to be, supernatural occurrences but have always managed to ignore them or push them to the back of my mind. However, the experience on Mount Sinai was too powerful to ignore or to suppress.

From my university studies, I knew that mystical experiences were universal, reported by members of every faith and religion throughout history. How valid could my mystical experience be when millions of Hindus report similar encounters? I know some of my Christian friends would say the Hindus worship powerful demonic forces that imitate the mystical experiences of the true God to trick people into worshipping them. I think a more Jewish explanation would be that the one true God can touch the lives of people of diverse faiths who interpret these experiences through their own filters. I decided I did not need to explain away the experiences of others for my own to be valid. What I needed to do was interpret it through the filter of Scripture rather than my own human wisdom.

One of my favorite passages in the Bible is the 13th chapter of Deuteronomy, which I take as my touchstone for how to relate to genuine supernatural events. It talks about a prophet who performs genuine signs and miracles but teaches us to worship other gods. We are not to listen to that false teacher because:

> …the LORD your God is testing you to know if you really love the LORD your God with all your heart and all your soul.[1]

The verse immediately prior to the section on the false prophet says:

> You shall diligently do all the matter that I command you; you shall not add to it or diminish from it.[2]

In Christian translations, this verse is at the end of chapter 12, disconnected from the section on the false prophet in chapter 13. However, in Jewish sources, it is the opening verse of chapter 13 and understood as setting the context for the section on the false prophet. According to this Jewish understanding, it is a warning not to listen to anything or anyone that adds to or takes away from the commandments of God, even if it is someone who can perform genuine signs and miracles. I realized that any mystical experience that added to or took away from Scripture would be something I could not accept, no matter how convincing and miraculous it seemed or indeed was.

I started to think about the Biblical context of what happened that morning, experiencing God's love in such a tangible way. It was a *fatherly* love that enveloped me and cared for me. Relating to God as Father was something I never really connected with until a few years earlier, when I began to study what Christians refer to as the "Lord's Prayer." At the time, I was researching the Hebrew origins and meaning of that prayer together with a close friend and

---

[1] Deuteronomy 13:3[4] [NRSV].
[2] Deuteronomy 12:32[13:1].

colleague, Keith Johnson. We eventually wrote a book together about our findings called *A Prayer to Our Father.*[1]

The title of the book spoke volumes about the process I personally went through. When we started out, I couldn't connect to a prayer that addressed God as "Our Father in heaven." It sounded to me like a very Christian way to refer to God. Christians think of God in terms of a "Father" and a "Son," something that is completely incomprehensible to me as a Jew. Keith is a United Methodist pastor, and when we started researching the "Lord's Prayer," I thought of it as his prayer. I was along for the ride as a textual scholar and Hebrew expert. However, as our research progressed, I came to view it as a Jewish prayer I could embrace. After all, Jesus was a Jew and he taught this prayer to a Jewish audience in the Land of Israel. The more we studied the "Lord's Prayer," the more I realized this prayer was completely Jewish. This was especially true of praying to God as "Father." Our joint study uncovered numerous Jewish sources that referred to God in His role as Father. One of the most significant was the "Song of Moses" in the Book of Deuteronomy, which said:

> He is your Father, your Creator; He made you and established you.[2]

The Song of Moses is the *only* section of Scripture every ancient Israelite was commanded to memorize at a time when many were illiterate.[3] This means that God's role as Father is not some peripheral metaphor but instead a core Biblical concept important enough to be included in the Song of Moses and learned by heart by every Israelite man, woman, and child.

I suppose my difficulty in relating to God as Father had its origins in the strained relationship I had over the years with my own, earthly father. My dad was an Orthodox Jewish rabbi. When I informed him as a teenager that I decided to embrace the faith of the Karaite Jews he was upset. The word "Karaite" comes from the

---

[1] Nehemia Gordon and Keith Johnson, *A Prayer to Our Father*, Hilkiah Press 2009.
[2] Deuteronomy 32:6.
[3] Deuteronomy 31:19.

Hebrew word meaning "Scripturalist." As the name implies, Karaite Jews believe the Hebrew Bible—what Christians call the Old Testament—to be the perfect Word of God. On the other hand, Karaites consider the teachings of the rabbis as nothing more than the opinions of men. To my father, this was utter blasphemy. By denying the holiness of rabbinical teachings, I was rejecting what he believed to be a core part of God's revelation to Israel. My father had been grooming me to become a rabbi, and my new Karaite beliefs were a huge disappointment to him. As I have matured and studied, I have come to appreciate the great wisdom contained in the words of the ancient rabbis, even though I do not accept them as binding. However, as a teenager I was not so open-minded and tended to emphasize the negative. This put additional stress on our relationship. Not only did I deny the teachings of the rabbis, but I openly ridiculed them. Over the years, my father and I both mellowed and came to tolerate one another's differences, but for many years our relationship was tense.

Whatever my issues were with my earthly father, researching the "Lord's Prayer" with Keith made me realize how important God's role as our heavenly Father was in the Hebrew Bible. By the end of that process, it was not only Keith's prayer to his Father; it was truly a prayer to *our* Father. This was something I came to believe deeply and had been traveling around teaching for the past two months. Up at the top of Mount Sinai I now experienced God as my Father for the first time, feeling His love in a tangible way.

As I made my way down the mountain, I brushed into some pilgrims wrapped in old blankets rented from the Bedouin the night before. In these tight quarters, a pungent smell of wool mixed with body odor filled my senses. It triggered a memory buried deep in the back of my mind. It was a memory of standing next to my father as a young boy, covered in his woolen *talit*, his prayer shawl. We were in our neighborhood synagogue on one of the high holidays. I could hear the chanting of the *kohanim*—Aaronic priests – standing at the front of the synagogue, pronouncing a string of Hebrew words over the congregation. I immediately recognized it as the *Birkat Kohanim*, the "Priestly Blessing" from the Book of Numbers:

> May the LORD bless you and protect you.
> May the LORD shine His face towards you and be gracious to you.
> May the LORD lift His face towards you and give you peace.[1]

I always knew my father loved me, but that was one of the few times during my childhood that I experienced his love. Whatever the issues were between us, standing with him under his *talit*, I felt covered in my father's love. This was the feeling I experienced up on the mountain, covered in God's love.

As these thoughts raced through my mind, I suddenly realized I had experienced the Priestly Blessing up on the mountain. After giving the descendants of Aaron the blessing to proclaim over the people, God concluded that section in the Book of Numbers:

> And they shall place My name on the children of Israel and I will bless them.[2]

This was precisely what the Kenyans did in their song. They placed God's name on me when they proclaimed Hallelujah, "Praise Yah," and I was blessed by God as I'd never been blessed before.

When I reached the bottom of the stairs, the human traffic jam dispersed, and I started walking briskly along the mountain trail. It occurred to me how much easier it was to walk down in the light of day than it had been to stumble up to the peak in the dark of night. The spiritual significance of this quite literally *dawned* on me. I had crossed over on dry ground, leaving behind heartache, and was now walking free from the bondage of sadness on the other side.

As I continued along the mountain trail, I breezed past some candles that had been illuminating one of the Bedouin way stations throughout the night. The candles were now burning out in the brisk early morning air, sending foul smoke wafting into my nostrils. This new smell triggered a second memory, one of Sabbath candles

---

[1] Numbers 6:24–26.

[2] Numbers 6:27. The passage opens with a commandment for Aaron and his descendants to proclaim the blessing, which is reiterated in Deuteronomy 21:5.

oozing smoke as their wicks extinguished in a puddle of melted wax. This was a familiar smell from my childhood; every Friday night at my family's Sabbath evening dinner my father would go around the table and bless all the children. I was always third, after my two older sisters. He would place his right hand on my head and recite a blessing taken from the Book of Genesis: "May God make you as Ephraim and as Manasseh."[1] He would then continue by reciting the Priestly Blessing from the Book of Numbers. Every Friday night, fathers all over the Jewish world bless their children in this manner. My heart raced as I suddenly realized the Priestly Blessing truly is a Father's blessing to His children. The blessing is a wonderful gift bestowed upon us by our heavenly Father. I had spent a great deal of time uncovering the Hebrew origins of the "Lord's Prayer," an ancient *prayer* to our Father. At that moment, I knew I needed to do the same thing with the *Priestly Blessing*, to uncover the Hebrew meaning of this ancient benediction that both Jews and Christians recite in their respective worship services, *a blessing from our Father*.

---

[1] Genesis 48:20 [NKJV]. Because he was not a *kohen*, a priestly descendant of Aaron, my father would only place one hand on my head during this ceremony instead of two.

Chapter 2:

The Little Things

The low, quiet whisper came from somewhere down in the dust-covered road. It was the day after my experience on Mount Sinai, and my exploration of the Priestly Blessing had already begun. I was back at Nuweiba where the Israelites crossed the Red Sea and was walking down the main street at the southern end of town. It was little more than a dirt path running along the sea. Clusters of straw huts were punctuated by run-down shops selling trinkets to the swarms of Western tourists. Earlier that day, I walked to the nearby Bedouin residential district in search of fresh fruits and vegetables. Instead, I found a shop full of rotting produce crawling with maggots. On my way back, I saw children in rags playing among the barren, sandy dirt of the Sinai Desert, and it broke my heart. Now, I was looking for bottled water when I heard a mysterious voice coming from unknown quarters.

As I scanned my surroundings looking for the source, I suddenly spotted an adult male no more than three feet tall. He was a "little person," barely towering over a stack of bottled water. There was a deep sadness on his face as he motioned to me with his tiny twisted arm, trying to get me to buy his wares. Suddenly I was struck with the opening words of the Priestly Blessing, "May the LORD bless you." Looking at the miniature Bedouin man, I realized how profoundly God has blessed me, affording me opportunities some people never have.[1]

Seeing the little person reminded me of a life-changing experience I'd had a couple of years earlier in the Dominican

---

[1] Numbers 6:24.

Republic. My weeklong stay in the capital of that Third World country left me overwhelmed by the conditions in which millions of people lived. I remember sitting in the *barrio* in Santo Domingo during one of the nightly blackouts, hearing the moans of a little girl suffering the effects of drinking polluted water. I'd seen poverty on television and in movies, but until I was there in the thick darkness, smelling the stench of raw sewage flowing through the streets, I didn't really understand what poverty was. I actually thought of myself as poor, living in a tiny Jerusalem apartment without many luxuries.

What moved me more than anything was a discussion I had with a young Dominican man who told me how his brother was picked up by the National Police while he innocently walked down the street.

"What did he do?" I asked.

"He didn't do anything," the young man snapped back quickly.

"Yes, I know, everyone is innocent," I said sarcastically, placing air-quotes around the word *innocent*, "but what was he accused of?"

"Nothing," the young man insisted. He explained that the police were overworked and underpaid so they randomly nabbed people off the street and held them for ransom, or as it was officially known, "bail." No one dared complain about the polluted water, the electricity shortages, the dilapidated roads, or the piles of uncollected garbage, because they didn't want to end up being held for "bail."

That night, in the dark gloom of the island of Hispaniola, I offered up a prayer to God, thanking Him for the immense wealth I never realized I had. I live in a country where I enjoy an abundant supply of clean and cheap drinkable water, have access to a steady flow of electricity, and perhaps, most importantly, enjoy a high level of personal security. I'm never afraid the police will snatch me off the street and hold me for ransom. True, I have to deal with terrorism from time to time. That's part of life in my *barrio*. Nevertheless, I feel safer in Jerusalem than I ever did growing up in Chicago and certainly much safer than I did during my short time in the Dominican Republic. I can walk around my neighborhood in the middle of the night and there is nothing to make me afraid. I may not have a fancy car or lots of shiny stuff but God has blessed me abundantly.

Before my visit to the Dominican Republic, I took all these things for granted. I used to mope about in my perceived poverty, not seeing the riches that were right in front of my eyes all along. Until that night in the *barrio,* I was suffering from what I call the "*spirit* of Saul." Born into one of the poorest families in Israel, Saul became the first king of the twelve tribes. Yet his own sense of inadequacy prevented him from appreciating God's immense blessings. When Saul and David would return from battle, the women of Israel used to come out of the towns and villages and sing about their valor:

> Saul has smitten his thousands and David his tens of thousands.[1]

As King of Israel, Saul should have felt honored that the women were praising him for standing up to their Philistine persecutors. He should have felt equally honored that the women sang the accomplishments of David, one of the top warriors in his army. Instead, Saul was jealous and complained:

> To David they gave tens of thousands and to me [they] only [gave] thousands.[2]

Saul was a mighty warrior loved by the Israelite masses. His "thousands" accounted for more Philistines than the legendary warrior Samson slew in his entire lifetime. Yet Saul failed to appreciate this and was jealous that the women of Israel attributed more victories to his subordinate, David. Through his own negativity, Saul turned the compliment of the women of Israel into an insult.

I have to confess that throughout much of my life I have been as pessimistic as King Saul. I am sometimes impressed with my own capacity to find the grey lining in every cloud. I inherited this from my father. He was always a perfectionist. I remember I once got a 97

---

[1] 1 Samuel 18:7.

[2] 1 Samuel 18:8.

on a major test at Hebrew University. When I told my father about the grade he responded in a disappointed tone, "What happened to the other three points?" He turned my success into a failure through his negativity. My Dominican experience changed me. It made me realize I was laboring under the *spirit* of Saul with this type of thinking.

What really helped me see how blessed I am, occurred when my Dominican hosts complained about the problem their nation was facing with illegal immigration from the neighboring country of Haiti. They told me that over one million Haitians illegally crossed the border to get a "better life" in the Dominican Republic.

"If they are coming to get a better life in the Dominican Republic," I thought to myself, "how bad must things be in Haiti?"

This was a few years before the major earthquake that ravished that country and I can't even imagine how bad things are there now. Compared to the living nightmare that was Haiti, the abject poverty of the Dominican Republic looked like paradise.

The Haitian immigration problem illustrated to me how much being blessed has to do with perception. It brought to mind a wonderful proverb recorded in *Ethics of the Fathers*, a profound collection of early rabbinical wisdom:

> Who is a rich man? He who is happy with his portion.[1]

The point of this proverb is that a person who appreciates what he has is by definition wealthy. Unfortunately, most people think they need vast sums of money to make them happy. Solomon explained how futile this thinking is in the Book of Ecclesiastes:

> He who loves money will not be satisfied by money and he who loves abundance [will not be satisfied] by increase.[2]

Loving money and abundance is a recipe for failure. You can never satisfy these desires, no matter how much you amass. This proverb reminds me of the movie *Office Space*, the story of a low-level paper-pusher in a large corporation. When the protagonist dreams of

---

[1] *Ethics of the Fathers* 4:1.

[2] Ecclesiastes 5:10[9].

having a million dollars, his best friend asks him what he would do with all that money.

"I would relax. I would sit on my [rump] all day. I would do nothing," the protagonist excitedly announces.

His friend hears this and laughs, "You don't need a million dollars to do nothing. Take a look at my cousin; he's broke and don't do [nothing]."[1]

Of course, I'm not saying people should sit on the couch all day and avoid hard work. Solomon also said:

> All hard work brings a profit, but mere talk leads only to poverty.[2]

Persistent hard work with integrity will eventually yield fruit and lead to prosperity. However, if you don't appreciate that fruit, you'll never be happy no matter how much you acquire. I learned in the Dominican Republic, one of the poorest places on earth, that the secret to being rich is not to amass money or possessions, but to work hard and appreciate whatever blessings God bestows upon you.

Solomon made this point when he concluded his discussion on the love of money and wealth by saying that those who "enjoy their toil, this is a gift of God."[3] In other words, having a job you love is in itself a blessing, irrespective of how much money you earn from it. This is exactly what the protagonist in the movie *Office Space* discovered. After unsuccessfully trying to steal a million dollars and risking his freedom in the process, he learned that vast amounts of money are not what he needed to be happy. What he needed was good, honest work that didn't make him miserable. He ended up trading his corporate cubicle for a shovel and hardhat at a construction site. He wasn't a millionaire living out his fantasy of sitting on the beach sipping margaritas all day, but he was content with life.

In contrast, his co-worker Milton, who stumbled upon the stolen million dollars, actually did sit on the beach sipping margaritas

---

[1] *Office Space*, directed by Mike Judge, 1999.
[2] Proverbs 14:23 [NIV].
[3] Ecclesiastes 5:19[18].

all day. Yet he was miserable in this tropical paradise because he was a miserable person unable to appreciate what he had. The movie ends with Milton in his beachside lounger fuming that there was too much salt in his margarita. I look back on all this now and sometimes wonder if I'm like Milton, living in one of the wealthiest countries on earth, complaining that there is too much salt in my proverbial margarita.

There's a great modern-day proverb that expresses how much being blessed has to do with our own self-perception. "You can never be too rich or too thin," the saying goes.[1] Many people, especially women, think they need to lose weight regardless of how skinny they are. Some will starve themselves to death trying to achieve their "ideal" body weight. The problem with many of these women is not their weight but the self-perception of their weight. The same thing is true of many people when it comes to money and possessions. There are millionaires who will work themselves into a coronary. No matter how much they have, they always think they need more. I realized how true this was from my Dominican hosts who were some of the happiest people I ever met. Despite their economic and material hardships, they appreciated what they had: loving families and good friends.

Looking closer to home, my own mother has been bound to a wheelchair from the age of two after surviving polio—a disease now virtually extinct. Nevertheless, she is one of the most capable people I have ever met and never let her handicap defeat her. Although she can't walk, she appreciates what she has and considers herself blessed. In retrospect, I suppose I shouldn't have felt bad for that little person selling water alongside the dirt road in Nuweiba. For all I know, God may have blessed him with a loving family and granted him the wisdom to appreciate what he has.

I've learned a great deal about appreciating God's blessings in my own life from my dog Georgia. She was a Rhodesian Ridgeback, a type of dog originally bred in southern Africa to hunt lions. Besides battling felines, this breed is notorious for looking hungry. No matter

---

[1] This quote is attributed to Wallis Simpson.

how much you feed a Ridgeback, they always look like they are on the verge of starvation. Georgia also happened to drool a great deal and preferred human food to her own canine gruel. Whenever I would sit down for a meal, she would come scrambling into the room so fast she sometimes tripped over her own legs. She would then beg at my feet for a taste.

One time Georgia had to wear an "Elizabethan collar," those cone-shaped things they put on a dog's neck to prevent them from licking an open wound. When I had dinner that night, Georgia sat at attention waiting for her "tithe" with the collar pointing at me like a satellite dish. About-half way through my meal, I looked down to see the collar overflowing with saliva. The pooch had half-drowned herself in drool.

On one of my first speaking tours, I had to leave Georgia behind in Jerusalem. I started to notice that the flavor of everything I ate was off. Something was missing. I realized that food tastes better when a ferocious Lion Dog is begging for a morsel. Her apparent desperation for even the tiniest scrap made me appreciate every bite so much more.

It's human nature to appreciate things more when they are valued by others, even a dog. This made me realize that I should appreciate every blessing God gives me, whether it is another breath in this world or a single day with the woman I truly love. It's so easy to take these things for granted. When I fall into this trap, I try to think of my hungry hound's hankering for my home cooking. I've learned to appreciate when God looks down on me and throws me a tiny scrap. I hope He forgives my nagging. He knows we humans are a breed that always looks hungry no matter how much He feeds us.

Chapter 3:

Rebooting My Biblical Faith

Sweat dripped down my brow as I furiously jotted notes on a piece of paper. It was over a decade before my experience at Mount Sinai and I was about to have my first life-changing encounter with the Priestly Blessing. I was sitting in a classroom struggling to concentrate on the words of the bald-headed, raccoon-eyed professor as he droned away in academic Hebrew. I was living my dream, studying at the Hebrew University of Jerusalem.

I remember only a few years earlier wondering if I would ever understand Hebrew well enough to carry on a basic conversation. Now, here I was listening to a lecture on the history of the Biblical text from a native-born Israeli speaking in the language of the prophets. As the lecture concluded, the professor announced that next time he would talk about something he called the "Secret of the Twelve." He promised that this would be the key to unlocking the mysteries of the Bible. I was so excited I had to take a deep breath just to calm myself. One of the top scholars in Biblical studies, a master of ancient languages and archaeology, was going to reveal to *me* the secrets of the Bible!

When I arrived for class later that week, I was bursting with excitement. I got there twenty minutes early just to make sure I didn't miss a single word. As I waited for class to start, I thought about my computer, an old 486sx that ran the notoriously unstable Windows 3.11 operating system. One day I was clicking around on my old computer when I suddenly found myself inside an application called "File Manager." As I clicked and tapped, I periodically noticed strange little files that I didn't recognize. These phantom files all seemed to end with a period followed by the three letters "ini." I decided that these "ini" files were a waste of space on my 256-megabyte hard-drive so I started deleting them. The next day, when I tried to boot up my computer, I was in for a shock. It turned out that these "ini" files contained vital information that Windows needed to run. Desperately, I took my computer into a lab. Through herculean efforts, they were able to salvage my data but the techie admonished me, "Stay out of File Manager. It's not for novices." Now I was sitting in a classroom at the Mount Scopus campus of the Hebrew University and any moment now a Bible "techie" was going to fill me in on the mysteries of Scripture's very own "File Manager."

When the lecture finally started, the professor explained that the *Secret of the Twelve* first appeared in the writings of a 12th Century rabbi named Abraham Ibn Ezra. When I heard the name of this rabbi, it caught my attention. One of my favorite past-times was studying the Bible, and even as a Karaite, I developed a great respect for this particular rabbi, considering him as one of the greatest Bible commentators of all time. According to the professor, Ibn Ezra's "secret" was that Moses was *not* the author of the Torah.

When the professor said that Moses didn't write the Torah, I was shaken to my very core. Growing up in an Orthodox Jewish home, I struggled for years with the validity of what the rabbis call the "Oral Law." I was taught from a young age that when Moses went up to Mount Sinai, he received two bodies of revelation. The first was the Torah consisting of the Five Books of Moses. The second body of revelation, I was taught, was the Oral Law supposedly preserved by the rabbis down through the ages.

As I studied the Oral Law, it seemed to me to be nothing more than the opinions and doctrines of later rabbis and not true Mosaic revelation. At the time, I never even questioned the validity of the written Torah. I just took it as a fact of history that God revealed every single letter of Genesis through Deuteronomy to Moses. Now, one of the top Bible scholars in the world was telling me that I had been duped about the written Torah as well.

In his lecture, the professor claimed that the Torah was pieced together from four separate "documents." Each of these documents was supposedly written by a different ancient group that had its own opinions and doctrines about the nature of God and His plan for mankind. This meant that the Torah of Moses—Genesis, Exodus, Leviticus, Numbers, and Deuteronomy—was really written by four bickering religious factions. When the professor said this, I suddenly had the sensation that my entire world was collapsing around me. Everything I held dear and on which I based my life was a lie. I had uprooted my life, moving to Israel, because I believed God gave my ancestors the Holy Land as a precious gift. If what the professor said was true, I had based my decision on a fairy tale. What made it worse was that Ibn Ezra, a 12th Century rabbi I highly respected, was supposedly confirming it was all a fairy tale. I felt like the protagonist in the movie *The Truman Show* when he found out he was living his entire life in a reality TV show, and everyone he ever met was conspiring to keep this truth from him.[1]

I took a few days to recover from this news. When I finally came out of the shock, I decided that no matter how much I admired and respected the professor, it would be a mistake to accept blindly what he said. His claims were only as valid as his proof. What I needed to do was to look at the evidence for myself. At the same time, part of me was afraid to consider the possibility that he was right. Surely, it was blasphemy to question the divine authorship of Scripture. After much thought and prayer, I decided that I needed to know the truth, whatever the outcome might be. The true blasphemy would be to leave these questions un-asked.

One afternoon I sat down and pored over the commentaries of Ibn Ezra. As I investigated the *Secret of the Twelve*, I found out it actually had to do with "anachronisms" that Ibn Ezra found throughout the Five Books of Moses. An anachronism is something in one period that really belongs to a later period. One of my favorite examples is in the Mel Brooks film *History of the World Part I* when a man swaggers into the ancient Roman forum with a boom box pressed up against his ear blasting the song "Funky Town."[2] Brooks

---

[1] *The Truman Show*, directed by Peter Weir, 1998.
[2] *History of the World: Part I*, directed by Mel Brooks, 1981.

introduced this anachronism to be funny but there was nothing funny about finding anachronisms in the Bible.

One major anachronism Ibn Ezra found was when Abraham chased a band of raiders "as far as Dan."[1] The problem was that "Dan" only got its name years after the death of Moses when the Tribe of Dan conquered the city of Laish and renamed it after their ancestor.[2] Ibn Ezra pointed out that Moses could only have called the city "Dan" if he were writing through prophecy, using its *future* name. When I read this, I thought about those ridiculous time-traveling scenarios in the *Back to the Future* movies. I imagined Biff Tannen knocking on my head and shouting, "Think, McFly, think!"[3] Tannen was right; that didn't make any sense.

My next step was to start investigating other anachronisms in the Torah. I eventually came across a discussion in the Talmud on the last chapter of Deuteronomy describing Moses' death. Moses could not have written about his own death in the past tense, so this was an obvious anachronism. The Talmudic rabbis refused to accept this and instead explained that Moses wrote prophetically about his own demise. "God dictated and Moses wrote with tears," the rabbis concluded.[4] I could just imagine what Biff Tannen would say about this. As I kept reading I found out some of the ancient rabbis shared my apprehension. They found it hard to believe Moses would write about the future in the past tense and determined *Joshua* wrote the last *eight* verses of Deuteronomy.

It turns out that this was the key to Ibn Ezra's *Secret of the Twelve.*[5] According to Ibn Ezra, Joshua wrote all *twelve* verses in the last chapter of Deuteronomy.[6] The chapter opens with Moses going up to Mount Nebo where God shows him the Promised Land "as far as Dan." Ibn Ezra reasoned that if Joshua were responsible for the anachronistic reference to Dan in the last *twelve* verses of Deuteronomy, then he must also be responsible for anachronisms

[1] Genesis 14:14.
[2] Judges 18:29. See also Joshua 19:47.
[3] *Back to the Future*, directed by Robert Zemeckis, 1985.
[4] *Babylonian Talmud*, Baba Batra 15a [Soncino translation].
[5] See Ibn Ezra on Deuteronomy 1:2.
[6] See Ibn Ezra on Deuteronomy 34:1.

throughout the Torah. In Ibn Ezra's time, it was controversial enough to attribute the last twelve verses of the Torah to Joshua—earlier rabbis only dared attribute eight verses to him. Anything beyond this was unthinkable. In one passage, Ibn Ezra warned his readers, "it is a secret and he who is wise will remain silent."[1]

As I investigated Ibn Ezra's secret, I realized he was not calling into question the Mosaic authorship of the Torah, as my professor had claimed. He was merely pointing out that Joshua wrote the odd phrase or verse here and there, after the death of Moses. I still struggled with this and understood why Ibn Ezra kept it a secret. Indeed, when I shared the first draft of this chapter with some friends, they urged me not to include it in the book. They insisted on maintaining the secret even today. My friends were concerned that letting people know that Joshua had a part in writing the Torah would shake their faith.

I'm not a big believer in secrets. I think the truth needs to come to light no matter how difficult it may be for some people to process. If your faith is built on a lie or half-truth, then what good is it anyway? Now, I have to admit that I was a little shaken myself when I first realized *Joshua* wrote some of the verses of the "Torah of *Moses*." However, as I searched for answers I discovered this was something Scripture itself states quite clearly. In the Book of Joshua, it says:

> And Joshua wrote these words in the Book of the Torah of God…[2]

The "words" that Joshua wrote in this context consisted of the renewed covenant the nation made with God in the last chapter of the Book of Joshua. If Joshua could write those words "in the Book of the Torah of God," then it is not contrary to Scripture to say he also wrote other words in the Torah. After all, Joshua wasn't just any old prophet. He had a special role when God revealed Himself to

---

[1] See Ibn Ezra on Genesis 12:6.
[2] Joshua 24:26.

Moses in the desert. The Book of Exodus talks about the tent Moses set up outside the camp where God would speak to him:

> The LORD would speak to Moses face to face, as one man speaks to another. And he would then return to the camp; but his attendant, Joshua son of Nun, a youth, would not stir out of the tent.[1]

While Moses was having this unique form of revelation, speaking to God *face to face*, Joshua was sitting there in the tent right next to him. If anyone was qualified to write in the Torah, it was Joshua. I am not suggesting Joshua added or changed commandments. That would violate the clear commandment in Deuteronomy not to add to or take away from the commandments revealed through Moses.[2] However, Joshua may have updated information in the Torah for his generation, such as changing "Laish" to "Dan."

My investigation into the *Secret of the Twelve* left me confident in the Five Books of Moses, Joshua's prophetic contributions notwithstanding. However, my professor's challenge to the validity of the Torah didn't end with Joshua. In a series of lectures, he expanded on something called the "Documentary Hypothesis." This is a theory of secular scholars who believe the Torah is comprised of four contradictory "documents." It starts with the observation that the Book of Genesis has two supposedly contradictory descriptions of the creation of the world. According to the Documentary Hypothesis, these two accounts were each written by a different rival group with its own unique understanding of Creation.

After the class that night, I closely read the opening chapters of Genesis. I saw that what my professor called the "First Creation" (Genesis 1:1–2:3) described the Universe formed out of nothing in six days. In contrast, his so-called "Second Creation" (Genesis 2:4–25) did not refer to the number of days.

"Why was the world created twice?" my professor sarcastically asked the class earlier that day.

---

[1] Exodus 33:11 [NJPS].

[2] Deuteronomy 4:2; 12:32[13:1].

As I now re-read the passages closely, I questioned my professor's claims. The way I read it, the so-called "Second Creation" was actually part of the story of the Garden of Eden in the following chapter. In modern texts, the Garden of Eden story in Genesis chapter 3 is disconnected from what appears to be a "Second Creation" in Genesis chapter 2. However, the division into chapters did not exist until the 13th Century. In the original Hebrew, Genesis chapter 2 continues into chapter 3 as a continuous unbroken text. This means that the "Second Creation" in Genesis 2 is not really about Creation. Rather, it is setting the scene for how the first humans arrived in the Garden of Eden, which ultimately led to their banishment. What my professor saw as two contradictory creations were really dealing with two different issues: Creation in Genesis 1 and the Garden of Eden in Genesis 2–3. Each section had its own focus and hence provided different sorts of details.

Beyond the alleged contradictions, the bigger issue my professor emphasized was the different names of God in the two sections. "It is common knowledge," my professor explained, "that the First Creation account calls God *Elohim* while the second one calls Him *Yahweh*." According to my professor, the fact that the two sections use different names for God proved that two rival religious factions wrote them.

It wasn't in my nature to take his word for it. I had to see for myself. When I looked closely at the "names" for God, I saw he was right about the "First Creation." It consistently called the Creator *Elohim*, a Hebrew word meaning "God." However, what he called the "Second Creation"—actually the "Garden of Eden"—didn't quite fit what he was saying. It used the Tetragrammaton, the holy name of God written with the four Hebrew letters Yod-Hay-Vav-Hay, roughly equivalent to the English "YHVH." But this was always followed by the title Elohim, identifying YHVH as Elohim—God. Additionally, the Garden of Eden story used Elohim all by itself without YHVH in four instances. This completely contradicted the picture my professor had presented. Both sections quite clearly referred to God by His title Elohim and the second one even identified Elohim by His personal name YHVH. The claim that these two sections called God by different names may have been *common knowledge*, but it was *factually untrue.*

Even after discovering the holes in the Documentary Hypothesis, it was difficult for me to dismiss it. After all, it had the authority and weight of the great luminaries of modern Biblical research who I admired and respected. I found myself up late at night wondering if all these great professors could be wrong. In the months to come, I spent countless hours reading every word of the Torah, trying to give the Documentary Hypothesis the benefit of the doubt. Yet repeatedly, the hypothesis created to explain textual difficulties in the Torah ended up creating more problems than it supposedly solved.

The deathblow to the Documentary Hypothesis came the following semester during a course on ancient Hebrew inscriptions. Another professor presented a pair of tiny silver scrolls discovered in a burial cave in Jerusalem. When the silver scrolls were first unrolled back in the early 1980s, archaeologists saw that they were inscribed with Paleo-Hebrew letters. Paleo-Hebrew is the original Hebrew alphabet used by Moses and all the early prophets up until the Babylonian Exile in 586 BCE. When the Jews returned to Israel under the leadership of Ezra around 450 BCE, they brought many Babylonian influences back with them including a foreign alphabet. Ezra trained as a scribe in Babylon and started using the Aramaic alphabet to write Hebrew. This turn of events was a great historic irony. Aramaic started out as a corrupt and confused form of Hebrew, created when God mixed up the languages at the Tower of Babel. After exile in Babylon, the Jews started using the Aramaic alphabet to write Hebrew. The bastard-child of Babylon was being used to write the original language God spoke when He commanded the Universe into existence. Until this very day, Hebrew newspapers, street signs, and even Bibles are written in the Aramaic alphabet. The importance of the two silver scrolls from the burial cave in Jerusalem is that they predate all this corruption and confusion.

As scholars started to decipher the two silver scrolls, they immediately recognized the Priestly Blessing from the sixth chapter of the Book of Numbers. That was the same blessing I encountered as a child in the synagogue covered with my father's prayer shawl and would years later experience for myself up on Mount Sinai. Both scrolls contained this ancient blessing, making them the oldest surviving copies of any Biblical text. The professor pointed out that the earliest *complete* manuscript of the Hebrew Bible was only about a thousand years old. The Dead Sea Scrolls contained even earlier *fragments* dating back about 2,300 years. The two silver scrolls with the Priestly Blessing predated the earliest Dead Sea Scrolls by 350 years. This made the Priestly Blessing the oldest copy of any Biblical passage to survive the ravages of time.

I knew the silver scrolls had profound significance for the Documentary Hypothesis. One of the cornerstones of that hypothesis was the existence of the so-called "Priestly Source" of the Torah. This Priestly Source was supposedly written by a group of priests concerned with the rules and regulations of the Jerusalem Temple. There could be no greater example of a priestly document than the Priestly Blessing itself. According to the Documentary Hypothesis, the Priestly Source wasn't written until *after* the exile when Ezra arrived back in Jerusalem around 450 BCE. *If the Documentary Hypothesis were true, the earliest copy of the Priestly Blessing should be no older than 450* BCE *and written in the Aramaic alphabet that Ezra brought back with him from Babylon.* The two silver scrolls debunked this theory. They dated to 650 BCE, before the Babylonian Exile, and contained the original Paleo-Hebrew writing.[1]

After the lecture on the two silver scrolls, I was so excited that I rushed across town to the Israel Museum. The professor had shown us photographs and diagrams of the scrolls but now I was standing in front of the originals, on display behind a sheet of plexiglass. Chills spread throughout my body as I thought about how these tiny scrolls contained the very same blessing God delivered to Aaron and his

---

[1] Recent photographs of the silver scrolls have revealed another biblical passage, an excerpt from Deuteronomy 7:9, which further weakens the Documentary Hypothesis. According to the hypothesis, a Priestly passage should not exist alongside an excerpt from Deuteronomy before the Babylonian Exile. See Gabriel Barkay, Marilyn J. Lundberg, Andrew G. Vaughn, Bruce Zuckerman, "The Amulets from Ketef Hinnom: A New Edition and Evaluation," *Bulletin of the American Schools of Oriental Research*, volume 334 (May 2004), pages 41–71.

sons 3,500 years ago. Aaron's direct descendants have been proclaiming the same three verses, the same fifteen Hebrew words, the same sixty letters ever since without missing a single day.[1] The basic ritual hadn't changed substantially in all those centuries. Now I was standing in front of the two oldest surviving copies of this ancient benediction.

I bent over and strained to read the tiny letters but couldn't decipher much. I knew the archaeologists used advanced imaging techniques to photograph and decipher these tiny scrolls, but I wanted to see what I could read with my own two eyes. I don't know how long I stood there as I struggled to read each letter. I was eventually able to make out one Hebrew word, and my legs went weak when I realized what it said. It was God's holy name, the Tetragrammaton, written out with the four Paleo-Hebrew letters: Yod-Hay-Vav-Hay.

As I stood there looking at God's name on the silver scrolls, I was in awe but also a little perplexed. I never noticed the name of God in the Priestly Blessing. I read that section of Scripture dozens of times and even knew it by heart. I ran through the blessing in my head but the name of God never cropped up, not even once. Yet there it was in Paleo-Hebrew on the silver scrolls. I suddenly realized why the name was missing from my memory of the blessing. I was raised with the tradition that God's name was too holy to speak. Whenever I came across the name in Scripture, I was taught to replace it with the title *Adonai* meaning "Lord." In the synagogue as a child, covered with my father's prayer shawl, the *kohanim* always proclaimed the Priestly Blessing with the title Adonai—Lord—and this was how I remembered it. I was suddenly feeling like Truman from that movie again. I pulled my Bible out of my backpack and flipped to the section on the Priestly Blessing. The name of God was right there in black and white, three times, once in each line of the blessing. As I read the concluding verse of that section, my heart

---

[1] I grew up in an Ashkenazic Jewish community where the Priestly Blessing is only pronounced in the Diaspora on high holidays, but in many Jewish communities, it is pronounced daily.

skipped another beat. After giving Aaron and his descendants the blessing, God proclaimed:

> And they shall place My *name* on the children of Israel and I will bless them.[1]

These words made me think about that ancient Israelite scribe who painstakingly etched out the Priestly Blessing on the two tiny sheets of silver. It was all about the blessing of God's name. His dying wish was to be buried in his family tomb with these silver scrolls so that God's holy name would be placed on him and his loved ones for all eternity. He was covered with God's holy name just as I had been covered with my father's prayer shawl. This made me realize the key to unlocking the mysteries of Scripture wasn't about splitting hairs over whether Moses or Joshua or some other prophet wrote this verse or that word. It was about being covered with the blessing of God's holy name. At some unknown point in the ancient past, someone erased the "ini" files, teaching His people to swap out His name with a substitute. It was time to restore File Manager and reboot my understanding of the Bible.

---

[1] Numbers 6:27.

Chapter 4:

And They Shall Place My Name

I really liked two things about the Hebrew University library. The first was the air-conditioning. After making Aliyah—immigrating to Israel—it took me quite a few years to adjust to the oppressive, dry heat of Jerusalem. The main library at Mount Scopus always had the air-conditioning turned up a little too high and it reminded me of the biting-cold winters of Chicago where I grew up. The second thing I liked was the carpet. I know they installed it to reduce noise, but I loved the way the fibers softly crunched under my feet. It reminded me of stomping on virgin snow in the "moon boots" my mother bought me in second grade.

I was at the library looking for answers. Seeing God's holy name in the Priestly Blessing inscribed on the ancient silver scrolls left me troubled. I stayed up all night thinking about generation after generation of priests proclaiming the blessing without speaking God's name over the people. I wanted to understand where things had gone wrong. This was years before the invention of Google so I had to do good, old-fashioned book research.

I started out in the library catalogue looking for information on the Hebrew phrase *Shem HaMeforash*. In English, this is usually translated as the *ineffable name*, which means the "unspeakable" name. However, *Shem HaMeforash* actually means the "explicit" or "unequivocal" name. Ancient Jewish sources refer to God's actual name as the *Shem HaMeforash* to distinguish it from God's numerous titles such as "Lord," "Holy One," etc. God's personal name is usually referred to as the *Tetragrammaton* in English—the four-letter name—because it is written with the four Hebrew letters Yod-Hay-Vav-Hay (YHVH). Rabbinical tradition teaches that the

Tetragrammaton is too holy to use in common speech and prayer. As a result, whenever Orthodox Jews see God's name they systematically replace it with one of His titles. At the time, I was not questioning this tradition. What I had a problem with was extending it to the Priestly Blessing. The Book of Numbers said, "and they shall place *My name* on the children of Israel."[1] Surely, this meant proclaiming God's actual name over the people.

As I researched the subject of God's holy name, I quickly found that I wasn't the only one who read the passage in Numbers this way. The Talmudic rabbis, commenting on this section of Scripture, said:

> "Thus shall you bless the children of Israel"—It means with the Tetragrammaton (*Shem HaMeforash*). You ask, is it really with the Tetragrammaton or with a title? Scripture says, "And they shall place My name." My name which is unique to Me.[2]

The very same rabbis who were telling me to replace the Tetragrammaton with one of God's titles in common speech and prayer insisted that the Priestly Blessing had to be recited using God's actual name. Using the Tetragrammaton was crucial, because it was how the priests placed God's name on the people. A little more research and I found Ibn Ezra, the same 12th Century Bible rabbi who spoke about the *Secret of the Twelve*, also shared this view. In his commentary on Numbers, Ibn Ezra wrote:

> "And they shall place My name"… it means that they will mention My name over them, because the great and awesome name is in every one of the three verses [of the blessing].[3]

I was pleased to see that Ibn Ezra read the verse the same way I did. Even though he lived a thousand years after the Talmudic rabbis, I had tremendous respect for his mastery of the Hebrew language and his intellectual honesty.

---

[1] Numbers 6:27.

[2] *Babylonian Talmud*, Sotah 38a quoting Numbers 6:23 and 6:27, respectively.

[3] Ibn Ezra on Numbers 6:27.

While I felt vindicated in my reading of the passage in the Book of Numbers, I was even more confused now. I couldn't understand why no one used the Tetragrammaton in the Priestly Blessing if everyone agreed that is what the Bible said to do. I got a partial answer as I continued my research. In the writings of the early rabbis, I came across a description of the way the Priestly Blessing was performed in the days of the Second Temple:

> How is the Priestly Blessing performed? … In the Temple they say the name the way it is written and outside the Temple they use a title.[1]

According to these rabbis, the Priestly Blessing was only to be pronounced with the Tetragrammaton *in the Temple.* Outside the Temple, a substitute for the Tetragrammaton had to be used. This was the answer: No Temple, no Tetragrammaton. Then again, this didn't really answer the question; it only framed it. Where did the rabbis get the idea that the actual name of God could only be used in the Temple?

As I read on, I found that the rabbis themselves did not seem to know the origin of this practice. In the Talmud, they struggled to find a source for it and tried to read it into various Scriptural verses. One sage, named Rabbi Josiah, who lived in the middle of the 2nd Century CE, tied it to a verse in Exodus where God said, "in every place where I cause My name to be mentioned, I will come to you and bless you."[2] Rabbi Josiah explained:

> Do you think it really means in *every* place? Rather, this verse is scrambled. It should read, "In every place where I come to you and bless you, there will I cause My name to be mentioned." And where do I come to you and bless you? In the Temple. There, in the Temple, I cause My name to be mentioned.[3]

---

[1] *Mishnah*, Sotah 7:6. See also *Mishnah*, Tamid 7:2.
[2] Exodus 20:24 [NJPS].
[3] *Babylonian Talmud*, Sotah 38a.

Rabbi Josiah understood the promise that God would bless the people "in every place where I cause My name to be mentioned" to be a reference to the Priestly Blessing. This made him uncomfortable because it implied the Priestly Blessing was to be pronounced with the Tetragrammaton "in every place." Rabbi Josiah solved this problem by *rearranging* the words of the verse, thereby giving it the exact opposite meaning. This was precisely the type of interpretation that made me choose the Karaite path. It wasn't "exegesis"—deriving meaning from the verse. It was "eisegesis"—reading meaning into the verse. What bothered me so much was that Rabbi Josiah obviously understood the plain meaning of the verse but still decided to rearrange the words to fit his preconceived beliefs.

As I read Rabbi Josiah's interpretation of Exodus, I became even more convinced that the Priestly Blessing needed to be recited with the actual name of God. God Himself caused His name to be mentioned by commanding the priests to pronounce the blessing in His name. This reminded me of something my father told me in the synagogue as a child. He said the reason for covering ourselves with the *talit*—prayer shawl—during the Priestly Blessing was so that we wouldn't look at the priests and think that they were the source of our blessing. They were only pronouncing the words, but God was blessing us. God is the only one who really has the power to bless us. It seemed to me that this was exactly what God was saying in Exodus. He will come to every place He causes His name to be mentioned, to every place where the priests proclaim the blessing in His actual name, and He will bless us Himself. What an amazing promise! This is a promise not limited by time or location. It applies to "every place," wherever a blessing is made in God's actual name, not just the Temple.

I needed a break after a long morning of poring over books in the university library, so about midday I headed over to the cafeteria for lunch. While I was waiting in line for my schnitzel, french fries, and rice, I ran into an old friend, an Orthodox Jew who was also studying at the university. I told him about my research to find out why the Priestly Blessing wasn't pronounced using God's name.

He nervously adjusted his *kippah* and gave me a funny look as if I had just said something stupid. "Of course the *kohanim* use God's name!" he protested. "That's what it's all about. They raise their hands and proclaim God's name over the people." When he said they used "God's name," he was referring to the divine title Adonai meaning "Lord."

I responded with a funny look of my own and told him the Tetragrammaton, Yod-Hay-Vav-Hay, was the only "name" of God. "All the rest are just titles," I announced incredulously.

On my way back to the library it occurred to me that I had made a pretty bold statement to my Orthodox friend, and, in retrospect, I wasn't really sure if it was true. If I was going to be honest with this inquiry, I would have to look up every single time the Hebrew word for "name" appeared anywhere in the Bible and examine each and every one in its context. Back then, the only way to do this was with *Mandelkern's Hebrew Concordance*, a fat, dusty book containing every word in the Bible, arranged according to its grammatical root with a Scriptural reference. When I got back to the library, I went straight for the burly volume and got to work. There were 881 verses to examine. This would take me days.

The work was painstaking, but the results were worth it. Through many hours of research, I confirmed that none of God's numerous titles—such as *Holy One*, *Most High*, or *Lord*—were ever referred to in Scripture as God's "name." Even El Shaddai, usually translated as "God Almighty," was nothing more than a *title.* Whenever the Hebrew Bible talked about God's "name," it was always referring to the Tetragrammaton, YHVH. There was only one possible exception. A verse in Isaiah says:

> You O YHVH are Our Father Our Redeemer from everlasting is Your name.[1]

There were two ways to read this verse, depending on where you put the commas, semicolon, and capital letters. Of course, ancient

---

[1] Isaiah 63:16. Psalms 68:4[5] refers to "Yah" as God's "name," but this is a poetic abbreviated form of the Tetragrammaton, not a separate name.

Hebrew did not have commas, semicolons, or even capital letters, so this was clearly a matter of interpretation:

> *Interpretation #1:* You, O YHVH are Our Father, "Our Redeemer from everlasting" is Your name.
> *Interpretation #2:* You, O YHVH are Our Father, Our Redeemer, from everlasting is Your name.

According to the first interpretation, God's name is "Our Redeemer from Everlasting." Most English translations and some Jewish Bible commentators read it precisely this way.[1] The problem is that this would be the only place in the entire Hebrew Bible where our heavenly Father has a second "name" besides the Tetragrammaton. The second interpretation, that God's name YHVH is "from everlasting," made more sense to me.[2]

My research at the library left me with more questions than answers. I was troubled more now than when I started. I decided to head over to the Nachlaot neighborhood of Jerusalem to visit a friend forty years my senior. He was a Karaite Jew named Mordechai who immigrated to Israel from the United States decades earlier. Moredechai came from a rabbinical background similar to mine and struggled with many of the same Biblical issues with which I was now struggling. By profession, he was a diamond cutter, and he read the Bible with the same exacting precision that he used to cut diamonds. Mordechai reminded me of "Morpheus," the character in the movie *The Matrix* who mentored the young protagonist, Neo. In a key scene, Morpheus offered Neo a choice between swallowing a red pill that would cause him to know the truth and a blue pill that would cause him to forget they ever met. Morpheus warned Neo that the truth might be very unpleasant, and that once he swallowed the red pill, there would be no turning back. Mordechai's red pills came in the form of simple Scriptural truth that shook my blissful world of ignorance to its very core. He never let me take anything for granted

[1] This is the interpretation of the traditional Jewish commentator Metsudat David and English translations such as NJPS and the Stone Edition.

[2] This is the interpretation of the traditional Jewish commentator Radak and the English translation KJV.

and always challenged me to support my assumptions with Scriptural facts. If anyone could help me get answers, it was Mordechai.

I paced back and forth in Mordechai's tiny living room as I told him about the silver scrolls, about the name of God written in Paleo-Hebrew, and about the rabbis saying that the Tetragrammaton could only be spoken in the Temple. Mordechai sat there perched on the edge of an old wooden stool, listening quietly.

When I was done with my monologue, Mordechai looked up at me and asked me in a calm, authoritative voice, "Why stop there?"

I wasn't sure what he meant.

"Why only use the name of God in the Priestly Blessing?" he elaborated.

I wasn't sure where he was going with this. "God's name is too holy to use in any other context," I confidently replied. Even as the words came out of my mouth, I knew what was coming next.

"Where does it say that in the Bible?" Mordechai asked with a raised brow. It was a rhetorical question. He knew it didn't say that anywhere. And he knew that I knew that too.

The next thing he did was classic Mordechai. He told me to open up my Bible to the 3rd chapter of Exodus and start reading aloud. This was it. The red pill. It wasn't too late to choose the blue pill and walk away. However, I knew that I would never be satisfied with the blue pill, so I sat down, swallowed hard, and started reading the chapter in Hebrew. It was about Moses and the burning bush. The interesting part came in verse 13 when Moses asked God to identify Himself by name:

> Behold when I come to the Children of Israel and say to them, "The God of your forefathers has sent me to you," and they ask me, "What is His name?" what should I tell them?[1]

Moses knew there were countless gods in ancient Egypt and he couldn't just say to the Israelites, "God has sent me to you." Even "God of your forefathers" was too ambiguous after four generations

---

[1] Exodus 3:13.

immersed in idolatry. The Israelites would demand to know which god. The answer appears in verse 15:

> And God said further to Moses, thus shall you say to the children of Israel, YHVH, the God of your fathers, the God of Abraham, the God of Isaac, and the God of Jacob has sent me to you, this is My name forever and this is My memorial from generation to generation. [1]

When I came to the Tetragrammaton, YHVH, I read it as I always did, as Adonai, meaning "Lord." This was the rabbinical tradition with which I was raised, and even as a Karaite, I never seriously questioned it. Mordechai didn't have to say anything. As I came to the end of the verse, I realized I had fundamentally changed its meaning by substituting God's actual name with "Lord." I had read it, "Lord… this is My name forever." This wasn't limited to the Priestly Blessing.

Even as the red pill hit my stomach, I resisted. "Does it really matter?" I questioned nervously. "I mean, God knows what we mean so why is this so important? Isn't it just enough to know what His name is without speaking it?"

Mordechai responded by telling me to read from the Book of Kings. It was a prayer that Solomon offered when he dedicated the First Temple:

> When Your people Israel are defeated by an enemy because they sinned against You, they shall return to You *and they shall confess Your name* and pray to You and ask for mercy from You in this Temple.[2]

The key words were "and they shall *confess* Your name." The Hebrew word for "confess" used in this verse was *hodu.* I knew this could also mean "and they will *praise* Your name." Either way, Solomon was saying we should *confess* or *praise* God's name in times of trouble. I thought about all the bus bombings and shootings. I needed to start praying with God's name.

---

[1] Exodus 3:15.

[2] 1 Kings 8:33.

Mordechai wasn't done. He pulled a dusty book off the shelf. It was a *Midrash*, an ancient collection of rabbinical homilies, on the Book of Psalms. The page he wanted was already dog-eared. He started to read:

> Why does Israel pray in this world but not get answered? Because they do not know the Tetragrammaton (*Shem HaMeforash*). However, in the future world the Holy One, blessed be He, will inform them of His name, as it is written, "Therefore, My people will know My name." At that time they will pray and be answered, as it is written, "He will call Me, and I will answer him."[1]

As Mordechai read this to me, I had a terrifying thought. Was God not answering our prayers, because we weren't praying using His name? I immediately thought of Majdanek. When I was a senior in high school, I went on a weeklong trip to Poland with thousands of other Jewish teenagers from all over the world. We came to learn about the Holocaust.

The tour began at the Umschlagplatz, the Warsaw train station where hundreds of thousands of Jews were loaded into cattle cars and sent to their deaths. I expected emotion to overcome me, but strangely, I felt nothing. Then came the death camps. Auschwitz and Treblinka. Names that strike fear in the heart of every Jew. Still nothing. Then Majdanek. I had never even heard of Majdanek. It was a death factory but was small compared to the more famous ones. The death toll at Majdanek was eclipsed by Auschwitz, where two million Jews perished. What made Majdanek stand out was that it was captured intact. At all the other sites, I saw memorials and placards. At Majdanek, I saw the machinery of death. The death camp looked very much the way it did in 1944 when Red Army tanks rolled up to its gates. There was a long warehouse full of shoes. Thousands and thousands of shoes. The Nazis didn't want anything to go to waste, so they stripped their victims before gassing them.

---

[1] *Midrash Tehillim* on Psalms 91:8 quoting Isaiah 52:6 and Psalms 91:15, respectively. This tradition is repeated in *Pesikta Rabbati*, section 22.

Each pair of shoes represented a victim. A human being. A Jew. As I stood there staring at the endless sea of shoes, I burst into tears. There was another teenager there, a girl. I didn't know her, but she was also crying. We ended up in an embrace. I cried. She cried. We held each other. I never knew her name. Never even saw her face. Just a boy and a girl comforting each other in the face of human tragedy. Now years later, I was wondering if we'd prayed to God in His actual name would the result have been any different? This seemed to be what the Midrash was saying.

On my way home from Mordechai's apartment, I couldn't stop thinking about all the suffering that the Jewish people have experienced over the last two thousand years: the pogroms, the forced conversions, the massacres. Then there was the future world the Midrash spoke of. This would be a world in which the suffering ended. A world in which the Messiah would sit on His throne as king of the earth. A world in which God's people will know His name, pray in His name, and their prayers will be answered. This reminded me of one of my favorite verses in the Bible, a verse that also speaks about that future world:

> For then will I turn to the people a pure language that they may all call upon the name YHVH, to serve Him with one shoulder.[1]

What I found fascinating about this verse was that it alludes to the curse of the Tower of Babel. The Book of Genesis relates that before the Tower of Babel, "the whole earth had one language and one speech."[2] Mankind used their common language to come together in rebellion against God proclaiming:

> Come, let us build ourselves a city, and a tower with its top in the heavens, *and let us make a name for ourselves…*[3]

God responded to this rebellion by mixing up their languages and scattering them across the earth. Zephaniah was promising that the

---

[1] Zephaniah 3:9.

[2] Genesis 11:1 [NKJV].

[3] Genesis 11:4 [NRSV].

curse of Babel would be lifted, that all mankind would once again speak a common language. At Babel, they stood shoulder-to-shoulder to make a name for themselves. Zephaniah was promising that in the future world, all mankind would stand shoulder-to-shoulder to proclaim the name of God. I now realized that this literally meant proclaiming His name, the Tetragrammaton, YHVH. Earlier that week at the library, I discovered that the Second Temple priests originally pronounced the Priestly Blessing with the Tetragrammaton. Now I was discovering that in the future world *all mankind* will call upon the actual name of God. The red pill was doing its work. The "world that had been pulled over my eyes to blind me from the truth" was fading.[1] It was time to see how deep the rabbit-hole went.

---

[1] *The Matrix*, directed by Andy Wachowski and Lana Wachowski, 1999.

Chapter 5:

Spiritual Mixing of Seed

The bright Jerusalem sun reflected off the white sheen of the tiny marble panels. I was standing in front of a 1:50 scale model of the Second Temple created by one of Israel's top archaeologists. I came to see what it might have looked like when the Temple priests proclaimed God's holy name over the people. With the image of the Temple replica still burning in my mind, I shut my eyes tight and was transported 2,000 years back in time. Standing among the jostling crowd, I angled to get a glimpse of the priests decked out in their sacred regalia on the wooden platform. The multitude became quiet when the high priest raised his arms. He then began the Priestly Blessing by pronouncing slowly and carefully the first word. *Ye-va-re-che-cha. May He bless you.* Hundreds of voices thundered in unison from atop the platform, repeating every syllable. The first word of the holy blessing echoed through the Judean hills and ascended up into the heavens.[1] Silence then gripped the Temple courtyard as the crowd held their breath in anticipation of the next word, God's holy name, the name revealed to Moses at the burning bush. Suddenly, the words I read in the Talmud echoed from somewhere in the back of the Temple courtyard:

> Is the Priestly Blessing really with the Tetragrammaton or with a title? Scripture says, "And they shall place My name." My name which is unique to Me.[2]

---

[1] See 2 Chronicles 30:27.

[2] *Babylonian Talmud*, Sotah 38a discussing Numbers 6:27.

The image of the Temple quickly faded as I opened my eyes, leaving me with a burning question: What was it about the Priestly Blessing that made God's "unique" name so important? I mean, what difference did it make if the priests blessed the people using one of God's titles?

I found the answer months later when re-reading one of my favorite passages in the Bible. It was the section in Genesis in which Abraham fought against the raiders who pillaged southern Canaan, the ones he chased "as far as Dan."[1] On his way back from this victorious battle, two Canaanite leaders—Melchizedek and the King of Sodom—approached Abraham. Melchizedek was a mysterious figure described as "a priest of the Most High God" who opened the meeting with a blessing:

> And [Melchizedek] blessed him saying, "Blessed is Abram by the Most High God, Creator of heaven and earth. And blessed is the Most High God who has delivered your enemy into your hand."[2]

I remembered learning that the Canaanites had a deity of their own called the "Most High God Creator of heaven and earth." They believed that this god created the Universe before retiring and turning it over to his son, Baal. Abraham knew Melchizedek was righteous and was referring to the same God he worshipped. But the King of Sodom was a notorious idolater and might understand the title "Most High God" as referring to the retired Canaanite creator-deity. When the King of Sodom offered Abraham great riches, the patriarch responded by using the same title for God that Melchizedek used, but with one small and important difference:

> And Abram said to the King of Sodom, "I lift my hand to YHVH, the Most High God, Creator of heaven and earth."[3]

---

1 Genesis 14:14.

2 Genesis 14:19–20.

3 Genesis 14:22.

Abraham didn't want the King of Sodom to think he was talking about the father of Baal so he added God's actual name, YHVH, to remove any ambiguity.

Abraham's encounter with the King of Sodom made me realize one of the powerful things about the Tetragrammaton is that it really is *unique* to the one true God. Titles like "Most High," "God," and "Lord" could refer to Baal, Zeus, Krishna, or a whole host of foreign deities. The name YHVH is unique to the God of Israel. It seemed to me that this was why God commanded the descendants of Aaron to proclaim the Priestly Blessing using His *unique* name—so everyone would know YHVH was the source of the blessing. There was an inherent risk in using an ambiguous title like "God" or "Lord" in that the blessing could mistakenly be attributed to a pagan deity.

I learned how serious this risk was from a passage in the Book of Samuel that described one of King David's major battles against the Philistines:

> And David came to *Baal-Peratzim* and David smote them there and said, "YHVH has burst forth (*paratz*) upon my enemies before me as the water bursts forth (*peretz*)," therefore he called the name of that place *Baal-Peratzim*.[1]

I was sitting in the Hebrew University library reading the Bible on my laptop when the significance of this verse struck me. Heads all over the library turned as I suddenly blurted out a spontaneous "uh-oh," the kind Dustin Hoffman blurted out in the movie *Rain Man* whenever something went wrong.

What I realized was that David was comparing his victory in this important battle to the flashfloods common in the Judean Mountains. When it rains, a wall of water can come washing through seasonal mountain creeks in a matter of seconds, sweeping away everything in its path. I've only witnessed this a few times and can testify that it is truly an awe-inspiring spectacle. David was saying that God burst forth upon the Philistines like a flashflood suddenly bursting forth in a dry mountain creek during heavy rain. The word

---

[1] 2 Samuel 5:20.

for bursting-forth is *paratz* and this is the source of the name of the battle-site: *Baal-Peratzim*. Here comes the "uh-oh." *Baal-Peratzim* means "Baal Bursting-forth!" David should have called the name of the place, *YHVH-Peratzim* (YHVH Bursting-forth) or *El-Peratzim* (God Bursting-forth) or even *Adonai-Peratzim* (Lord Bursting-forth). Instead, he gave the chief Canaanite deity, Baal, credit for the blessing he experienced in his victory over the Philistines.

I had trouble accepting this at first. I was raised with an idealized view of King David, a view expressed in the Talmudic dictum:

> Anyone who says that David sinned is in error.[1]

The rabbis who defended this view of a sinless David created excuses for all his apparent wrongdoings. He didn't really commit adultery with Bathsheba, they argued, because her husband, Uriah, gave her a provisional divorce when he went out to battle. Uriah, for his part, deserved to die, because he defied David's order to go back to his wife and re-consummate his lapsed marriage. The excuses continued until even some of the Talmudic rabbis tired of them. One rabbi acrimoniously quipped that those who justify David only do so because they are his direct descendants and want to glorify their own lineage.[2] In the interest of full disclosure, I have to confess that according to a family tradition, I am descended from King David on my mother's side. Despite this, I am not going to try to justify David's errors. He was not perfect, as David said of himself in the 69th chapter of Psalms:

> O God, You know my foolishness; and my sins are not hidden from You.[3]

Still, it was hard for me to believe David would name the site of his major battle after Baal. After all, he was a *mashiach*, a messiah. I don't mean the one we expect to come in the future and bring world peace. David was a *literal* messiah, which means, "anointed one." The prophet Samuel anointed him with oil, as it says:

---

[1] *Babylonian Talmud*, Sabbath 56a.
[2] *Babylonian Talmud*, Sabbath 56a.
[3] Psalms 69:5[6] [NKJV].

> Then Samuel took the horn of oil and anointed him in the midst of his brothers; and the spirit of YHVH came upon David from that day forward.[1]

In English, this might not sound like it has anything to do with a *messiah*. However, in Hebrew, when it says, "[he] anointed him," it uses the same root-word as *mashiach*, "messiah." You could legitimately translate this as "[he] made him a messiah" or "[he] messiah-ed him." Here's the thing: when Samuel anointed David with oil, at that very moment God anointed David with His own spirit, the "*spirit* of YHVH." Scripture says that God's spirit was with David "from that day forward." This means when David named the site of his important battle "Baal Bursting-forth," the *spirit of YHVH* was with him.

I was willing to adjust my assumptions to fit the historical and Scriptural facts. When David committed adultery with Bathsheba, tried to cover up his crime, and finally ordered Uriah to be murdered, God's spirit was also with him. Having God's spirit with you doesn't mean you lose your free will and it doesn't necessarily make you sinless.

David was anything but sinless. Flirting with idolatry was one of his perennial flaws. We get a glimpse of this when David was on the run from King Saul. On one occasion, Saul's men descended upon David's home to arrest him and he conveniently slipped out the window. As he fled, his wife Michal "took an idol and laid it on the bed; she put a net of goats' hair on its head, and covered it with the clothes."[2] Michal pulled the old dummy-in-the-bed trick, like in the movie *Escape from Alcatraz*.[3] The only difference was that she used a handy idol instead of a paper-mache head. My question was, "Why did David have an idol in his house?"

David's invocation of "Baal" wasn't a one-time, momentary lapse. I discovered that he actually named one of his sons after this

---

[1] 1 Samuel 16:13 [adapted from NKJV].

[2] 1 Samuel 19:13 [NRSV]. The word for "idol" in this passage is *terafim*, the same type that Rachel stole from Laban (Genesis 31:34). *Terafim* idols were apparently used for divination such as telling the future (Ezekiel 21:21[26]; Zechariah 10:2).

[3] *Escape from Alcatraz*, directed by Don Siegel, 1979.

false Canaanite deity. David was blessed with fifteen sons and one daughter whose names are listed in the Book of Samuel. His eleventh son appears in the list as Elyada, a perfectly *kosher* name comprised of two Hebrew words that mean, "God knows." The problem is that this wasn't the boy's real name. His real name appears when the list of David's sons is repeated in the Book of Chronicles as B'elyada, "Baal Knows."[1] *Uh-oh!*

David wasn't the only anointed King of Israel to name a son after Baal. Saul had a son who actually reigned as king over Israel for two years. The Book of Samuel gives his name as Ish-boshet.[2] This is a strange name for a king, because it means "Man of Shame." Why would Saul name his son "Man of Shame?" The answer is he didn't. His real name appears in the Book of Chronicles as Eshbaal, "Man of Baal."[3]

I was deeply troubled to find out David and Saul named their children after Baal. They knew YHVH was the one true God and that Baal was a false Canaanite deity. Why would they name their children after Baal? I found a clue in an obscure verse in the Book of Chronicles that listed some of David's warriors, who as it happens were disaffected relatives of Saul. One of these men was named B'elyah, a name that reveals what David and Saul were probably thinking. The name B'elyah could be translated as, "Yah is Baal." Yah is the poetic abbreviated form of YHVH's name, the one I heard on Mount Sinai, the one in Hallelujah. This warrior's name meant, "YHVH is Baal."

I realized from the name B'elyah that David and Saul didn't abandon the worship of the one true God in favor of the Canaanite deity, Baal. What they did was much more subtle and far more insidious. They referred to YHVH as "Baal," mixing the worship of

---

[1] 1 Chronicles 14:7. Evidently, the author of the Book of Samuel was not comfortable with the name Baal so he replaced it with *Boshet*, "shame."

[2] 2 Samuel 2:10.

[3] 1 Chronicles 8:33; 9:39. The Book of Samuel also changed *Yerubaal* "Let Baal Strive," Gideon's epithet after he destroyed the altar of Baal, to *Yerubeshet* "Let Shame Strive." *Boshet/ Beshet*, the Hebrew word for shame, was a standard replacement for Baal (2 Samuel 11:21; Judges 9:1; Jeremiah 11:13; Hosea 9:10).

the true God with the false worship of the Canaanites. They violated the verse in the Book of Leviticus, which says:

> You shall not sow your field with mixed seed.[1]

I'm not saying David and Saul engaged in forbidden farming practices. What they did was worse. They engaged in *spiritual* mixing of seed. When they named their children after Baal, they were calling YHVH "Baal."

Strictly speaking, Baal is not a name; it is a title meaning, "Lord." The actual name of the chief Canaanite deity was Hadad, but the Canaanites considered this an *ineffable name*. Only the priests of Hadad were allowed to speak his name in special rituals. Everyone else referred to Hadad by his primary title: *Baal*, "Lord." Herein lies the source for confusion: one of the legitimate titles of YHVH in the Hebrew Bible is Adonai, which also means "Lord." David and Saul probably equated Adonai and Baal and ended up referring to YHVH as "Baal." This was probably what David was thinking when he said, "YHVH has burst forth upon my enemies" and then named the site of his important battle *Baal-Peratzim*, Baal-Bursting-forth. When he said Baal, he was referring to YHVH as if He were Baal/ Hadad.

David and Saul weren't the only ones to identify YHVH with Baal/Hadad. I found a prophecy of Hosea that revealed this was a widespread error in ancient Israel. The prophecy said:

> And it shall come to pass on that day, says YHVH, you shall call Me "my husband" and you shall no longer call Me "my husband."[2]

When this verse translates literally, it doesn't make much sense. That's because in Hebrew it uses a play on words with two different terms for "husband." *Ish* and *Baal*. Baal means "Lord," but it can also mean "husband." God is saying, "You shall call Me *Ish-i* (my husband) and you shall no longer call Me *Baal-i* (my husband, my Baal)." The Israelites in Hosea's day were spiritually mixing seed, identifying YHVH with the chief Canaanite deity Baal/Hadad.

---

[1] Leviticus 19:19 [NKJV].
[2] Hosea 2:16[18].

God was not pleased with this and in the very next verse foretells a time when the speech of the Israelites will be cleansed of this spiritual seed-mixing:

> And I will remove the names of the Baals from her mouth,
> and they shall no longer mention them by name.[1]

Using God's unique name and avoiding pagan titles like Baal is a good start at staying away from spiritual mixing of seed, but it does not inoculate us against it. What makes spiritual seed-mixing so dangerous is that it's not your run-of-the-mill apostasy. David, Saul, and the Israelites of Hosea's day didn't abandon the faith in YHVH and outright convert to Baalism. They mixed the two faiths into an unholy hybrid. This was shocking to me. I had always been taught that idolatry would be something easy to identify, like a statue of the four-armed Indian elephant god Ganesh. No Jew in his right-mind would worship Ganesh. It's just laughable. But spiritual mixing of seed is much more surreptitious than presenting something that looks completely alien and abhorrent. It is a counterfeit faith. The thing about counterfeits is that they need to look like the real thing. A hundred-dollar bill featuring the portrait of Mad Magazine's Alfred E. Neuman would trick no one. The counterfeit needs to look real. Now dress up Ganesh in a *kippah* and *tzitzit*, hide his elephant trunk, and make him look like a righteous rabbi and you might get some people to worship him. The counterfeit deceives by taking the truth and mixing it with falsehood.

I decided to sit down and read the entire Hebrew Bible with this new understanding. I started to see the counterfeit faith as the major stumbling block of the ancient Israelites. The focus of this spiritual seed-mixing was the "high places" that the Israelites set up "on every high hill and under every leafy tree."[2] Most high places began as Canaanite places of worship that God commanded the Israelites to obliterate. Rather than destroy them, the Israelites converted them

[1] Hosea 2:17[19].
[2] 2 Kings 17:10.

into spurious temples where the worship of YHVH was freely intermingled with the worship of Baal/Hadad.

The prototype for these forbidden high places was the "House of God" built by a man named Micah. This wasn't Micah the Judean prophet who had a book named after him. It was Micah the Ephraimite in the time of the Judges who stole a large cache of silver from his mother. When he returned it, his mother said:

> I surely sanctify the silver to YHVH, from my hand to my son, to make a molten statue… and she gave it to a smith who made it into a molten statue…[1]

Micah's mother didn't dedicate her silver to Baal. In fact, Baal is not mentioned once in the entire story. Micah's mother dedicated the silver to YHVH and the statue made from that silver was presumably a *statue* of YHVH.

Micah's sin was classic spiritual seed-mixing. He took the manner in which the Canaanites worshipped Baal and used it to worship the true God YHVH. God specifically forbade this in the 12th chapter of Deuteronomy when He instructed the Israelites to destroy the Canaanite high places. After commanding the Israelites to tear down the Canaanite altars, smash their monuments, and burn their sacred-trees, God concluded:

> You shall not worship YHVH your God in such ways.[2]

This was a different sort of idolatry from what I had always been warned about. It wasn't about worshipping statues of false gods like Ganesh. God was commanding the Israelites not to spiritually mix seed by worshipping Him the way the Canaanites worshipped their deities.

As I explored the problem of spiritual seed-mixing in the Bible, I found that it emphasized three transgressions related to the high places. In addition to worshipping the true God through an idol, the prophets castigated the Israelites for *sacrificing* at the high places and

---

[1] Judges 17:3–4.

[2] Deuteronomy 12:4.

consecrating *non-Aaronic priests.* At first, I couldn't understand why these other two sins were important.

"Who cares," I thought, "about illegitimate sacrifices and imposter priests when the people are bowing down to an idol?"

As I dug deeper, I found that these other two transgressions were, Biblically-speaking, no less severe than idol-worship itself.

The problem with the sacrifices at the high places was that the Torah only allows them to be offered at "the place that YHVH chooses."[1] Originally, the chosen place was the mobile Tabernacle, but from the time of Solomon, God chose the stationary Jerusalem Temple.[2] According to Leviticus, anyone who sacrifices outside the Tabernacle or Temple, "the guilt of *bloodshed* shall be imputed to that man. He has *shed blood*; and that man shall be *cut off* from among his people."[3] Sacrificing at a high place was not just a trivial sin. Biblically it was considered tantamount to murder.

The problem with non-Aaronic priests is that only Aaron and his direct descendents were allowed to serve as *kohanim*, Temple priests. God commanded the Levites, direct descendants of Levi son of Jacob, to *assist* the *kohanim.* Any other Israelite who tried to carry out a Temple service was to be put to death.[4] Micah sinned by consecrating his own son, an Ephraimite, to serve as a priest. He later replaced his son with a Levite. While the Levites could carry out certain Temple functions, the Torah forbids them from serving as priests. This was an issue at the time of Moses when a Levite named Korah demanded that he be allowed to serve in the Tabernacle alongside Aaron. Korah and his disciples were swallowed up alive by the ground, showing God's displeasure for their rebellion. Micah's

---

[1] Twenty-five times such as Deuteronomy 12:5; 2 Chronicles 7:12.

[2] See 2 Kings 21:7; Ezekiel 43:7; 1 Chronicles 23:25; 2 Chronicles 7:16; 33:7.

[3] Leviticus 17:4 [NKJV].

[4] Numbers 3:5–10; 18:1–7. Accordingly, only Aaronic priests are permitted to proclaim the Priestly Blessing as part of the Temple service. However, nothing would prevent a layman from reciting this blessing outside the context of the Temple service. Jews traditionally respond to *kohanim* reciting the blessing with "Amen" whereas they respond *ken yehi ratzon*, "so may it be His will" when non-*kohanim* recite the blessing.

Levite erred in the sin of Korah by usurping the role of the Aaronic priesthood.[1]

Far from the control of the Tabernacle and later the Jerusalem Temple, and supervised by a counterfeit priesthood, the high places flourished as centers of spiritual seed-mixing where the worship of YHVH freely intermingled with the worship of Baal. The Book of Kings emphasizes the scope of this sin by mentioning for each King of Judah:

> …but the high places were not removed; the people still sacrificed and burnt incense in the high places.[2]

Surely, Solomon, who built the Temple in Jerusalem, was free of the sin of the high places. However, the Book of Kings says:

> And Solomon loved YHVH, walking in the statutes of David his father, but he sacrificed and burnt incense at the high places.[3]

Even Solomon was a spiritual seed-mixer.

After Solomon's death, his realm split into two kingdoms: Israel, representing ten northern tribes, and Judah, representing two southern tribes. The first monarch of the northern kingdom was Jeroboam, who made spiritual seed-mixing an official state institution. Jeroboam was afraid he would lose his kingdom if his subjects made their annual pilgrimage to the Temple in Jerusalem, which was controlled by his rival, the King of Judah. To prevent this, he set up two grandiose high places, one at Dan and the other at Bethel. At each of these high places, Jeroboam also consecrated non-Aaronic priests and a golden calf.

The first time I read about Jeroboam's golden calves, I thought he was an idiot for choosing such a loathsome symbol. Now, I realized how ingenious he was. In Jeroboam's day, people still remembered that their ancestors worshipped YHVH through a statue of a golden calf right after receiving the Ten Commandments at

---

[1] Numbers 16; Judges 17:5–10.

[2] 2 Kings 12:3[4].

[3] 1 Kings 3:3.

Mount Sinai. To strengthen the association with Mount Sinai, Jeroboam presented his two new idols with the exact words that the Israelites in the desert used to present their golden calf:

> Behold your God, O Israel, who took you up out of Egypt.[1]

I had to go back and re-read this several times to believe it. I was always taught that the golden calf was a statue of Baal. However, when read in context, I saw it was clearly meant to represent YHVH who took Israel up out of Egypt. Of course, the Torah tells us the golden calf was an abhorrent sin, but Jeroboam was not about to let a few Scriptural verses get in his way. There was a long-standing tradition of worshipping YHVH through a statue of a golden calf and he was going to take full advantage of it.

I was equally impressed with Jeroboam's choice of locations for his two high places. Dan and Bethel were at the northern and southern ends of his kingdom, making them accessible to everyone. Furthermore, Bethel was the site where Jacob had the dream of the ladder, and the Tabernacle was located there at one time.[2] Dan for its part had an ancient high place that traced back to the period of the Judges. Its non-Aaronic priests boasted an ordination that went back to Jonathan, the grandson of Moses.[3] Whatever Biblical verses the Judahite enemies might bring to undermine Jeroboam's high places, he had ancient venerable traditions on his side. If this doesn't warrant an "uh-oh" then I don't know what does.

Jeroboam's spiritual seed-mixing continued to plague the northern kingdom up until its destruction in 720 BCE. Meanwhile, in Judah, only two kings made any serious effort to stamp out the sin of the high places. The first was Hezekiah, whose attempt at eradicating this false worship really highlighted for me how deep spiritual seed-mixing ran in ancient Israelite society.

Hezekiah fought a desperate war of survival against the mighty Assyrian Empire when King Sennacherib invaded the Kingdom of

---

[1] 1 Kings 12:28 [compare NJPS and NAB]; compare Exodus 32:4, 8; Nehemiah 9:18.

[2] Genesis 28:19; Judges 20:18, 26; 21:2; 1 Samuel 10:3.

[3] Judges 18:30. In Hebrew, the name "Manasseh" is written with a "hanging *Nun*," revealing that it may have originally said "Moses."

Judah in 701 BCE. The Assyrian king sent his cupbearer, Rab-shakeh, to Jerusalem to demand Hezekiah's surrender. Hezekiah's ambassadors refused to submit, insisting they would be safe trusting in the God of Israel. Rab-shakeh responded with bewilderment:

> …when you say to me, "We trust YHVH our God," did not Hezekiah remove His high places and His altars and say to Judah and Jerusalem, "Bow down before this altar in Jerusalem."[1]

When I read this passage, I wondered how Rab-shakeh could have known that Hezekiah destroyed the high places. Judah was a backwater at the edge of the vast Assyrian Empire. I could see Rab-shakeh knowing about Judah's military strength or economic wealth, but this was an internal religious conflict of what was, to the Assyrians, an exotic and mysterious faith. This would be like the American president knowing what some minor Afghani mullah preached in his mosque on a Friday morning. The only way he could know this internal matter is if he had Judahite collaborators. Rab-shakeh's bewilderment must have reflected the attitude of his Jewish collaborators. These traitors were evidently upset that Hezekiah destroyed their beloved high places and considered him an enemy of YHVH for doing so. They laughed when the destroyer of their God's altars and high places said he was going to trust in that very same God.

This was a revelation for me. I had assumed those who worshipped at the high places would welcome Hezekiah's destruction of their false houses of worship. All he would have to do, I imagined, was read to them from Exodus, Leviticus and Deuteronomy, and they would fall down in repentance before dismantling the high places themselves. I was wrong. They saw Hezekiah as a persecutor and hated him for destroying their ancient altars. Hezekiah must have sounded like a maniac to them, quoting some obscure verses from the Torah that their ancient sanctuaries were a violation of God's will. I could just hear their objections to Hezekiah, "Why would God

---

[1] 2 Kings 18:22.

allow our high places to flourish for seven hundred years if they were against His will?" "Haven't these high places kept us together as a people for all these centuries?" The devotees of the high places must have seen the Assyrian invasion as a godsend. These foreigners had come to remove Hezekiah and to restore their ancestral worship. The story of Rab-shakeh made me realize that spiritual seed-mixers are devoutly dedicated to their counterfeit faith and that Scriptural facts mean little when compared to ancient traditions of worship. This was more than "uh-oh," it was "oy vay!"

After the death of Hezekiah, the high places came back vigorously. It wasn't until the time of his great-grandson, King Josiah, that the high places were eradicated. Josiah's campaign to cleanse Judah of these forbidden houses of worship met with stiff resistance. The Book of Kings reports:

> And [Josiah] desecrated the high places where the priests had burnt incense from Geva to Beersheba… But the priests of the high places would not come up to the altar of YHVH in Jerusalem and ate unleavened bread amongst their brethren.[1]

Rather than embrace the Scriptural truth Josiah was teaching, many of the Jewish multitudes and their non-Aaronic priests continued to practice their seed-mixing traditions, even after Josiah destroyed their illicit altars. *Major uh-oh!*

In the movie *Rain Man*, Dustin Hoffman's character was described as an "autistic savant." His doctor explained that he was obsessed with "routines, rituals, it's all he has to protect himself… any break from the routines and it's terrifying."[2] The priests of the high places in Josiah's day suffered from *spiritual* autism. They religiously followed their seed-mixing rituals, believing they were protecting themselves. When Josiah tried to force them to break from routine and follow Scripture, it terrified them. I don't want to be like Rain Man, stuck saying "uh-oh." I don't want to be like the

---

[1] 2 Kings 23:8–9.

[2] *Rain Man*, directed by Barry Levinson, 1988.

imposter priests of Josiah's day, bogged down in man-made routines and rituals. I don't want to be fooled by a counterfeit faith. As terrifying as it is, I am ready to tear down the high places in my life, trade in mixed seed for the real thing, and be blessed in God's unique and holy name.

Chapter 6:

The Burning Bush

Hundreds of slender stems covered with small tear-shaped leaves spilled down from a small crevice in the rock. The thick silence was broken by the sound of a spark. Then the crackling of wood wafting into the dry desert air. Soon, the bramble was engulfed in the glow of amber flames, luring the robe-clad shepherd to investigate. The bush burned with fire, but it was not consumed. It was in this setting that God first revealed His name to Moses.

Ever since reading about the burning bush with Mordechai, I was fascinated by this pivotal event in history. I couldn't get enough of it. I read books about it, admired paintings about it, and watched movies about it. One of my favorites was the classic Cecil B. DeMille film *The Ten Commandments*.[1] I rented it one year over Passover to watch with some friends. From the first scene, I was amused by the wild freedoms DeMille took with the story of Moses. As I sat on the couch munching on a piece of *matzah* (unleavened bread), I noticed the movie took especially great freedoms when it came to God's holy name.

The movie introduced the issue of the name in a scene about Moses discovering he was the son of a Hebrew woman, rather than of Pharaoh's daughter who raised him. Fearing Moses would lose his position of privilege in the house of Pharaoh, his Hebrew birth-mother initially denied her connection to him. Moses responded to this denial with a challenge, "Will you swear in the name of [your] God that you are not my mother?"

---

[1] *The Ten Commandments*, directed by Cecil B. DeMille, 1956.

Moses' mother refused the challenge insisting, "We do not even know His name!"

When I heard her say this, I choked, sending little bits of half-chewed *matzah* flying all over the living room. We don't even know His name? What was she talking about? The name of God, YHVH, appears 6,827 times in the Hebrew text of Scripture.

"What's not to know?" I wondered.

As I continued to watch the movie, the issue of the name kept coming up. In a second scene, Ramses was about to banish Moses to the desert for killing an Egyptian, when he declared in a skeptical tone, "I commend you to your Hebrew god who has no name."

In a third scene, Moses had just arrived in the tent of Jethro after miraculously surviving the perils of the desert. When Jethro heard about Moses' journey he announced, "He who has no name surely guided your steps."

"No name?" Moses replied, "You Bedouins know the God of Abraham!"

All three of these scenes were the product of the scriptwriter's imagination. If these events happened, Scripture did not record them.

The fourth and last reference to God's name in the movie was what really got my attention. It was the scene I had been waiting for, the reason I was watching the movie in the first place: the revelation at the burning bush. As I watched, I was sure I would finally hear the eternal name of God, the one I had encountered when I read the passage in Exodus aloud to Mordechai. Instead the movie faded to black just as God was about to reveal His name. I couldn't believe it. The most famous Bible movie ever leaves the God of Israel as "the god who has no name!"

I scrambled over to the bookshelf, pulled out a Hebrew copy of the Bible, and read over the 3rd chapter of Exodus. It was far worse than I thought. God revealed His eternal name to Moses in verse 15 but the movie ended the scene of the burning bush immediately after verse 14. This didn't leave God without a name. It changed His name to something else. I was sure this had to be the result of a bad translation. I quickly pulled a King James Bible off my bookshelf. It was one I "liberated" years earlier from a hotel bed-stand. Thank you, Gideons! I turned to Exodus chapter 3 and read the translation of verse 14 in English:

> And God said unto Moses, I AM THAT I AM: and He said, Thus shalt thou say unto the children of Israel, I AM hath sent me unto you.[1]

When Cecil B. DeMille saw the words "I AM" written in capital letters in the King James Version, he must have thought this was the eternal name of God. As I read on in the King James, I saw the name YHVH was absent from verse 15. Instead, it had the traditional replacement "LORD," written in capital letters. This was because the Christian translators learned Hebrew from rabbis who taught them the tradition of reading the Tetragrammaton as Adonai—Lord. Of course, "Lord" is not a name; it is a title. Seeing the title "LORD" in verse 15 must have confirmed to DeMille that God's eternal name was "I AM."[2]

I looked back over at the Hebrew and rolled my eyes. What DeMille missed is that "I am that I am" in verse 14 is the explanation of His holy name revealed in verse 15. In the Hebrew Bible, names are commonly accompanied by the explanation of their significance. Names were believed to encapsulate a person's nature, so these name-explanations had great importance. One of my favorite examples is a man named Jabez in the Book of Chronicles who received his name because his mother "bore him with sorrow." Jabez was terrified he would have a *jabez*-life, a life full of sorrow. So he prayed to God asking for prosperity and his prayer was answered.[3] The moral of the story is that even though a person's name encapsulates his nature, God is all-powerful and can bring prosperity, even to those otherwise destined for sorrow.

The Bible doesn't always come out and reveal the reason for a name. Sometimes it is simply implied by placing a related word in

---

[1] Exodus 3:14 [KJV].

[2] In a 2007 version of *The Ten Commandments* (directed by Bill Boyce and John Stronach), actor Elliott Gould in the role of God proclaims in a thinly veiled Brooklyn accent: "I am that I am. You will say, I am has sent me to you. This is My name forever and they will believe you."

[3] 1 Chronicles 4:9–10.

proximity to the name. A great example is Edom, the nation descended from Esau the brother of Jacob. When Esau was born, we are told he came out all "reddish." Anyone reading this in Hebrew knows that the name Edom means "red" and the significance of this name is that their ancestor was a "reddish" boy. Although Scripture never specifically says they were called Edom because of their ancestor's red hair, it is completely obvious in the original Hebrew.

When God said at the burning bush, "I am that I am," He was explaining the significance of His own name. The Hebrew word for "I am" is *Ehyeh*, derived from the Hebrew root meaning, "to be." In Biblical Hebrew, "I am" really means something like "I exist." By saying "I am that I am," God is declaring that He is the one who is, the one who really exists. He is different from the other gods who only exist in the imagination of men.[1]

God's name YHVH derives from the exact same Hebrew root as "I am." Strictly speaking, this name is a combination of three forms of this Hebrew root: *Hayah*, *Hoveh*, and *Yihyeh*. These three words mean, respectively: "He was," "He is," and "He will be." When we call Him by His name we are essentially saying, "He has always existed, He exists now, and He will always continue to exist." God says, "I am" about Himself but we are to call Him YHVH meaning, "He was, He is, and He will be." What all this means is that "I am" is not God's name; it is the explanation of His name. By ending the scene of the burning bush one verse too early, Cecil B. DeMille changed God's eternal name from YHVH—"He was, He is, and He will be"—to *Ehyeh*, "I am."

After watching the movie *The Ten Commandments,* I couldn't get the words of Moses' mother out of my head. I kept hearing her say, "We do not even know His name!" I thought back to the Midrash on the Book of Psalms that Mordechai read to me. It said Israel's prayers were not answered because we do not pray using God's actual name. I assumed the tradition to not use God's name in prayer was because His name was too holy. However, the Midrash was saying that the reason was "because they do not know the

---

[1] Isaiah 37:19; Jeremiah 10:1–11; Psalms 69:5; 115:4–8.

Tetragrammaton." It went on to say God would inform us of His actual name in the future world.

I knew that the consonants of the Tetragrammaton, YHVH, appear in the Hebrew Bible nearly seven thousand times. The uncertainty about pronouncing God's name had to be in the vowels. Hebrew vowels are written as a series of dots and dashes above and below the consonants. It is *common knowledge* that the Jewish scribes who preserved the Hebrew Bible swapped out the true vowels of God's name with the vowels of Adonai—Lord.[1] The Midrash seemed to be saying that the true vowels needed to pronounce the four Hebrew consonants Yod-Hay-Vav-Hay were a secret Israel would only learn in the future Messianic kingdom.

Without the vowels, there could be numerous ways to read the letters YHVH. I thought back to permutations in high school math class. Hebrew has eight basic vowels, plus a semi-vowel called *vocal-shva.* I wasn't sure where to go from there. I should have paid better attention in high school. Whatever the exact number, I knew the theoretical vowel combinations had to be in the thousands. Biblical Hebrew has certain rules that make the true number significantly lower, but it still had to be in the hundreds. Maybe Moses' mother in the movie was right. Maybe we didn't know God's name, at least not how to pronounce it.

As I investigated further, I found that some rabbis argued that God's name was a secret all the way back to the time of Moses. They found proof of this in God's statement to Moses at the burning bush, "this is My name forever." The Hebrew word translated as "forever" is *le-olam*, which literally means "for the Universe." When you say in ancient Hebrew that something is *le-olam*, "for the Universe," you are really saying it will continue to be true as long as the Universe continues to exist. When God said His name, YHVH, is *le-olam*, He meant that as long as the Universe continues to exist, this will be His name.

---

[1] "The divine name… has not its original vowels but those of Adonai…" *Gesenius' Hebrew Grammar*, section 102m.

The Talmud records a new interpretation of "this is My name forever" proposed by a 4th Century Babylonian rabbi named Nachman bar Isaac. This rabbi changed the vowels of the word *le-olam* "for the Universe" and instead read it as *le-[ha-]alim* "to conceal."[1] According to Rabbi Nachman, what God really said to Moses was, "this is My name *le-[ha-]alim*," meaning, "this is My name, to conceal."

When I read this in the Talmud, I let out a sigh of frustration. Was he serious? Even if I overlooked his modification of the vowels, it still did not make sense in the context. God started out saying to Moses in that verse, "thus shall you say to the children of Israel" and the next word was His holy name, YHVH. If God meant for Moses to keep His name a secret, then why did He tell Moses to reveal it to the children of Israel?

The Talmudic rabbis had an answer for this. They explained that Moses only revealed God's name to a select group of leaders who, in turn, only revealed it to their disciples. I thought back to the Priestly Blessing in the Book of Numbers, the one inscribed on those ancient silver scrolls in Paleo-Hebrew, the blessing that even the rabbis admitted had to be pronounced in the Temple using the sacred name of God. I wondered how the *kohanim* could have done this without revealing the secret to the Jewish multitudes gathered in the Temple. I stumbled across a fascinating report in the Talmud that, at the time, I thought answered this question. It was from a 1st Century CE rabbi named Tarfon who described how he performed the Priestly Blessing shortly before the Romans destroyed the Temple. Rabbi Tarfon explained:

> I once ascended the platform after my mother's brother, and inclined my ear to the high priest, and heard him swallowing the name during the chanting of his brother priests.[2]

---

[1] See *Babylonian Talmud*, Kidushin 71a and Rashi's explanation there.

[2] *Babylonian Talmud*, Kidushin 71a [Soncino translation]. Compare *Jerusalem Talmud*, Yoma 3:7 40d.

According to this, only the high priest used God's name during the Priestly Blessing in the Temple, and he pronounced it under his breath to prevent the masses from hearing it. After the Temple was destroyed, the secret continued to be passed down from rabbi to disciple, as a 4th Century rabbi explained:

> Sages transmit the four-letter name to their disciples once in a seven-year period.[1]

I didn't believe God intended Moses to keep His name a secret. Yet a secret it became all the same.

For several years, I had this deep desire to call on God's name but didn't know how to pronounce it. I examined numerous other scholarly theories and opinions but they were all just speculation and conjecture. Not a single one was based on any ancient Hebrew document.[2] I felt like Moses, cast out into the desert. I could just hear Yul Brynner's thundering voice saying, "I commend you to your Hebrew god who has no name."

I'll never forget the day this all changed. Two things happened that day. One of them changed my life and the other changed the world. It was back when I was studying for my Masters Degree in Biblical Studies and had a position as a researcher at the Hebrew

---

[1] *Babylonian Talmud*, Kidushin 71a.

[2] One theory I looked at based itself on the poetic form of God's name "Yah." This shortened form of the Tetragrammaton has crossed over into numerous languages as part of Hallelujah, Hebrew for "Praise Yah." While tradition forbade speaking the full name, there was never a prohibition against pronouncing this abbreviated form. Unfortunately, a "nickname" of this sort doesn't necessarily tell us how to pronounce the full form of the name. For example, a nickname like Mickey from Michael doesn't mean we should pronounce the full form of that name as "Mick-el." Nor does Jack from Jacob mean we should pronounce the full form as "Jack-ob." The same thing is true in ancient Hebrew; for example, King Azaryahu (Azariah) whose nickname was Uziyahu (Uzziah), not Azayahu (2 Kings 14:21; 2 Chronicles 26:1). Another theory I considered appears in the commentary of Rashbam, a 12th Century rabbi, who writes using a Hebrew cipher that the Tetragrammaton is to be understood as a variant form of the verb "to be" pronounced "Yihveh." While this rabbi was undoubtedly correct about the derivation of the name, this doesn't necessarily tell us how to pronounce it. Many Hebrew names are derived from verbs but their vowels rarely follow the exact patterns of those verbs. For example, my own name is derived from the verb *Nichem* "he comforted." Yet the proper pronunciation of my name is *N'chem*-yah not *Nichem*-yah. The most popular theory, that the name is to be pronounced Yahweh, is based on a second-hand Samaritan tradition reported by a 5th Century Christian author named Theodoret of Cyrus who didn't know Hebrew and was writing in Greek.

University Bible Project. The goal of the project was to compare systematically all manuscripts and ancient translations of the Hebrew Bible. As a starting researcher, I was assigned the worst job of all: proofreading the Bible.

I sat for countless hours with a printout of the Hebrew Bible spread out on a table alongside photographs of the Aleppo Codex.[1] Initially, I was excited. The Aleppo Codex is the most important manuscript of the Hebrew Bible in the world. All modern versions of the Hebrew Bible are based either directly or indirectly on the Aleppo Codex. This manuscript is so esteemed that it is housed in the "Shrine of the Book" in Jerusalem alongside the Dead Sea Scrolls. The Aleppo Codex was copied by hand by a master scribe in Tiberias who completed his work around 924 CE. Generations of Jewish scribes once traveled from all over the world to compare their Bibles to the Aleppo Codex, and I was following in their footsteps.[2] However, as I delved into the research, I found it to be more tedious than glorious.

Hebrew manuscripts of the Bible are swarming with countless dots and dashes, each with its own significance and meaning. Four sets of symbols exist on any given page of the Bible. I already mentioned the first two: the consonants and the vowels. The third set of symbols is the accent marks that guide pronunciation, serve as a simple system of punctuation, and guide chanting of the Bible in the synagogue. The fourth set of symbols is a complex system of proofreading notes used by ancient scribes to verify that the first three sets of symbols were copied correctly. My responsibility was to make sure that every little symbol was represented in the printed edition exactly as it appeared in the Aleppo Codex. It was a mind-numbing task. Some days I would sit for hours, and all I would find was a single, minor mistake. It gave me a great appreciation for those ancient Hebrew scribes who worked by candlelight to preserve every jot and tittle of the Bible.

---

[1] A codex is a handwritten manuscript in the form of a book, as opposed to a scroll.

[2] For example, the Leningrad Codex (folio 479a) was checked against the Aleppo Codex. See also Maimonides, *Mishneh Torah*, Hilchot Sefer Torah 8:4.

One day in the Autumn of 2001, I was proofreading the Book of Ezekiel, checking consonants, vowels, accents, and scribal notes. When I came to God's name, I noticed something special about the vowels, something that changed my life.

To explain what I found I need to back up and give some background. A few years earlier, I realized the importance of praying to God using His name but still didn't know how to pronounce it. In my search for the pronunciation, I started paying close attention to how various Hebrew printings of the Bible wrote God's name. The consonants were always the same, YHVH. The vowels were a different matter. I expected to find the vowels of Adonai in God's name. As I looked at numerous Bibles in Hebrew, I found that some of them had these vowels but not all of them. Some printers removed the vowels altogether as a shorthand way of telling the reader not to pronounce God's name the way it is written. There was no uniformity. The vowels of God's name had more to do with the whim of the printer than any ancient textual tradition.

One Hebrew Bible that caught my attention was a scientific edition I used for my university studies. It was a Bible printed in Germany called the *Biblia Hebraica Stuttgartensia* or BHS for short. What I liked about the BHS was that it was based on an important manuscript of the Bible in Hebrew called the Leningrad Codex. When I looked at God's name in the BHS, I noticed it never had the vowels of Adonai. The vowels of Adonai אֲדֹנָי are A-O-A (*chataf-patach–cholam–kamatz*)—the final "i" in Adonai is actually a consonant in Hebrew. Putting the vowels A-O-A into the consonants of God's name would create the hybrid form "Yahovah" יֲהֹוָה. However, I kept finding God's name written in the BHS as "Yehvah" יְהוָה with the vowels E-A (*shva–kamatz*).

Tetragrammaton with vowels of Adonai

Tetragrammaton in BHS

My experience with how freely the vowels of God's name changed in other Bible printings made me skeptical, so I decided I couldn't just rely on the BHS. This version was supposed to be based on the Leningrad Codex, and I needed to check this manuscript for myself. The Leningrad Codex was copied in Cairo around the year 1009 CE, making it the oldest surviving manuscript of the *entire* Hebrew Bible. Other manuscripts that were older did exist, but they were all missing sections. I wasn't about to fly off to Leningrad in Russia, but knew the university library had a facsimile edition with photographs of every page of the manuscript. A quick examination proved the BHS was faithfully reproducing the Leningrad Codex when it came to God's name.

As I examined page after page of the Leningrad Codex, it dawned on me just how big this was. The reason for all the uncertainty about pronouncing God's name was that the Jewish scribes supposedly inserted the vowels of Adonai into the consonants Yod-Hay-Vav-Hay. This was "common knowledge." However, "Yehvah" יְהוָה obviously didn't contain the vowels of Adonai. So it may have been *common knowledge*, but it was *factually untrue*.[1]

[1] The claim that the *chataf-patach* of Adonai was replaced with the *shva* of Yehvah to adapt it to the rules of Hebrew phonology ignores a basic rule of the Masoretic scribal system in which the vowels of the *qere* (marginal reading) are always inscribed in the *ketiv* (body of the text) *as is*, even when they create an otherwise impossible reading. A good example is the *shva* of the *qere* "*techorim*" inserted into the *ketiv* creating the impossible form *efolim*, resulting in an *ayin* vocalized with a *vocal-shva* (1 Samuel 5:9; 6:4). A more extreme example is the word *aleph-nun-vav* vocalized with the vowels of the *qere* "*anachnu*" (Jeremiah 42:6 on page 309 of the Aleppo Codex). The result is the impossible combination of a *shuruk* and a *vocal-shva* in a single *vav*.

There was one nagging problem with my new discovery. The vowels I found in the BHS and the Leningrad Codex were impossible. Pronouncing God's name as Yehvah יְהוָה defies a basic rule of Biblical Hebrew. In ancient Hebrew, a consonant in the middle of a word has to have a vowel associated with it. The problem was that the first *hay* in "Yehvah" יְהוָה did not have any vowel associated with it.[1] One common exception to this rule is a consonant that ends a syllable. In this case, the consonant is marked with a special symbol called a *silent-shva* to indicate that it has no vowel. For the pronunciation Yehvah יְהוָה to be valid, the first *hay* would have to be marked with a *silent-shva*.[2] It wasn't. This wasn't some minor glitch. It was the proverbial elephant in the room. Any ancient Hebrew reader who saw the word Yehvah יְהוָה written without a vowel or *silent-shva* in the first *hay* would know there was a *missing vowel* in God's name.

As time went on, my desire to figure out which vowel was missing from God's name grew. One day, I was reading my BHS Bible when I came across God's name written differently than it usually was. This time it had a full set of vowels. It was written: "Yehovah" יְהֹוָה.

This made so much sense, because it fit perfectly with numerous "compound names." Hebrew compound names consist of two

[1] A consonant that ends a word does not need to have an associated vowel. On the other hand, a *hay* at the end of a word is silent by default unless it is marked with a dot called a *mapik*.

[2] The only exceptions to this are three examples of compound names that begin with *lamed-hay* verbs, specifically: Asahel (2 Samuel 2:18), Pedahzur (Numbers 1:10), Hazael (2 Kings 8:8).

words that form a short sentence. Many of these compound names started with "Yeho," a truncated form of God's name. There was Yeho-shua, which means, "YHVH saves" and Yeho-natan "YHVH gives." There was Yeho-achaz "YHVH grabs hold," Yeho-chanan "YHVH is gracious," and Yeho-tzadak "YHVH is righteous."[1] The pronunciation "Yehovah" fit perfectly with these compound names.

I knew there was a second category of compound names that ended with "yahu," another truncated form of God's name. Some of these names had the exact same meanings as the other type. Like Yesha-yahu meaning "YHVH saves" and Netan-yahu "YHVH gives." There was also Achaz-yahu "YHVH grabs hold," Chanan-yahu "YHVH is gracious," and Tzidki-yahu "YHVH is righteous."[2] These names all ended with "yahu."

The two types of compound names had the exact same meaning, only differing as to where the three letters of God's holy name appeared in them. I saw a pattern. The *Yod-Hay-Vav* from God's name was always pronounced "Yeho" at the beginning of a name and "yahu" at the end of a name. In God's own name, these three letters were at the beginning, so Yeho-vah made perfect sense.[3]

HEBREW COMPOUND NAMES

Yeho-shua	Yesha-*yahu*	YHVH saves
Yeho-natan	Netan-*yahu*	YHVH gives
Yeho-achaz	Achaz-*yahu*	YHVH grabs hold
Yeho-chanan	Chanan-*yahu*	YHVH is gracious
Yeho-tzadak	Tzidki-*yahu*	YHVH is righteous

When I found the solitary instance of God's name written "Yehovah" יְהֹוָה in the BHS, part of me thought it might be a

[1] In English: Joshua (Exodus 17:9), Jonathan (Judges 18:30), Jehoahaz (2 Kings 10:35), Jehohanan (Ezra 10:28), and Jehozadak (1 Chronicles 6:14[5:40]).

[2] In English: Isaiah (2 Kings 19:2), Nethaniah (Jeremiah 36:14), Ahaziah (1 Kings 22:40), Hananiah (Jeremiah 36:12), and Zedekiah (1 Kings 22:24).

[3] No less an authority than Gesenius, who advocated pronouncing the name as "Yahweh" based on a Samaritan tradition, nevertheless admitted in his *Lexicon* (Tregelles translation, page 337): "Those who consider that יְהֹוָה [Yehovah] was the actual pronunciation… are not altogether without ground on which to defend their opinion. In this way the abbreviated syllables יְהוֹ [Yeho] and יוֹ [Yo], with which many proper names begin, be more satisfactorily explained."

misprint. I started scanning page after page, looking for another example. I spent about an hour but all I could find was God's name written Yehvah יְהוָה.

"What about the Leningrad Codex?" I thought.

I immediately knew what I had to do. I packed up my stuff and headed over to the library to examine, once again, the facsimile edition of the Leningrad Codex. On my way to the library I thought about why the scribes were writing the name as "Yehvah" יְהוָה even though it was obviously missing a vowel. They must have followed the tradition of not speaking God's actual name. By leaving out the middle vowel, they prevented their readers from accidently pronouncing it. When an ancient reader came across "Yehvah" יְהוָה, they immediately had to stop. Even if they wanted to read the name, it was unreadable because of the missing vowel.

When I arrived at the library, I set up my laptop on one of the tables and laid out the facsimile edition of the Leningrad Codex. When I was looking for God's name in the BHS, I had to skim manually page after page. Now I was going to take a short cut using a digitized text of the Leningrad Codex on my laptop. In a matter of seconds, a simple computer search turned up dozens of instances of the name of God, written as "Yehovah" יְהֹוָה with a full set of vowels. All I had to do was open to those verses in the facsimile edition and make sure that it really read that way in the manuscript.

Within a few minutes, I was looking at one of the most important manuscripts of the Hebrew Bible and there was God's name written numerous times, complete with all the vowels. And they weren't the vowels of Adonai. I couldn't believe it. Literally. I wasn't ready to believe it. I was having Gideon's doubt. In the Book of Judges, God gave Gideon a miracle, a dew-covered fleece on a dry threshing floor. However, Gideon wanted to be sure that it wasn't a fluke. He asked God for a second miracle, a dry fleece on a dew-covered threshing floor. I understood Gideon's heart. He was a Litvak like me. I needed to know that "Yehovah" יְהֹוָה with the full vowels wasn't a fluke, that it wasn't a quirk of the particular scribe who wrote this one manuscript. God's name was too important. I needed decisive proof.

Fast forward to the Autumn of 2001. I am sitting at my table at the Hebrew University Bible Project, proofreading the Bible. I am clutching a stack of photographs of the Aleppo Codex and painstakingly comparing them to a printout of the Hebrew Bible. And then I saw it. God's name with all the vowels. Complete. Nothing missing. It said "Yehovah" יְהֹוָה. Just at that moment, as I saw God's name with a full set of vowels in a *second* manuscript, my phone rang. I answered and the voice on the other end said, "An airplane just crashed into the World Trade Center."

The stack of photographs of the Aleppo Codex slipped out of my hands and scattered across the table. I asked if anyone was hurt. I was sure it must have been an accident. It happened before, back in the 1940s, to the Empire State Building. This was why tall buildings and towers had those flashing red lights. I didn't have access to the internet or radio and the caller did not have many details.

I put the phone down and took a deep breath. I needed coffee. I walked across the room to the kettle and mixed some Nescafé and non-dairy creamer into a mug of steaming water. I then sat back down at the table with my coffee mug, collected the stack of photos, and stared at God's name.

"It must have been an accident," I repeated in my head.

I decided to stop proofreading and furiously started scanning the photographs of the Aleppo Codex, looking only for the name of God. I kept finding the name written as "Yehvah" יְהוָה, the impossible form missing a vowel I had seen numerous times in both the Aleppo and the Leningrad. Then after about twenty minutes, I found it. A second instance of "Yehovah" יְהֹוָה in a *second* manuscript. This was decisive proof. It was my dry fleece on a dew-covered threshing floor. Then the phone rang. "A second plane hit the towers," the voice said in a troubled tone.

It wasn't a fluke. They were evacuating the towers. I put the phone down and swallowed hard. I thought about going home to watch the news, but I knew there was nothing I could do about it from Jerusalem, so I decided to continue scanning the manuscript.

I racked my brain trying to figure out why the scribes wrote "Yehovah" יְהֹוָה with a full set of vowels. Most of the time, they wrote it as "Yehvah" to prevent people from accidently pronouncing God's name. It was as if they occasionally slipped up and let out the secret they were supposed to hide. And then I realized that was exactly what happened. And I knew the reason for their indiscretion. It was something I was doing myself. Now that I knew how to pronounce God's name, I was reading it as "Yehovah" יְהֹוָה even when it said "Yehvah" יְהוָה in the manuscript. This was just something I did naturally. I didn't even think about it. Even when I read silently, I found myself "pronouncing" God's name in my head as Yehovah יְהֹוָה. I knew this sort of thing led to common typographical errors in English. It's the reason that expert spellers commonly confuse words like two, too, and to. They silently pronounce these words in their heads and end up typing the word the way it sounds, not the way it is supposed to be spelled. This must have been what happened to the scribes. The name was supposed to be a secret, transmitted from sage to disciple only once every seven years.[1] To maintain the secret, the scribes decided to withhold one of the vowels, writing the name as Yehvah יְהוָה. But rarely, less than 1% of the time, they slipped up writing God's name with a full set of vowels, as Yehovah יְהֹוָה, the way they pronounced it in their heads.[2] This also explained why the Leningrad Codex had the name written "Yehovah" יְהֹוָה dozens of times, but not in the same places as the Aleppo Codex. Both scribes occasionally blundered and wrote God's

[1] *Babylonian Talmud*, Kidushin 71a.

[2] When the Tetragrammaton follows or precedes the word "Adonai" (Lord), it is traditionally read as "Elohim" (God) to avoid reading Adonai twice in a row. When this happens, the vowels are usually changed in the Aleppo Codex from Yehvah יְהוָה (*shva–kamatz*) to Yehovih יְהֹוִה (*shva–cholam–chirik*), thereby cueing the reader to pronounce it as "Elohim." The scribe of the Aleppo Codex rarely withheld the "O" vowel from Yehovih, presumably because he knew this was not the true pronunciation of God's holy name. In contrast, the "O" of Yeh[o]vah (not juxtaposed to Adonai) was almost always withheld to prevent people from reading the name according to its true pronunciation. In one instance (Ezekiel 28:22), the scribe actually wrote the name as Yehovah יְהֹוָה even though it was juxtaposed to Adonai. This is significant because rather than inserting the vowels of Elohim, the scribe inserted the true vowels! The exact vowels of Elohim (*chataf-segol–cholam–chirik*) are only inserted in the name in one instance (יֱהֹוִה Zephaniah 1:7), proving there was nothing to prevent the scribes from vocalizing it this way throughout the Bible. Out of 295 instances preserved in the Aleppo Codex, the "O" is only withheld from the name juxtaposed to Adonai twice (Ezekiel 25:3; 37:21).

name the way they knew it was supposed to be pronounced. Just then, my phone rang a third time. The towers came down. Thousands died. I needed to go home.

That night, I watched those buildings collapse a thousand times on the evening news. The towers burned with fire and they were consumed. It was not the glowing amber flames of God's presence, but of evil, perpetrated under the false guise of faith. An old Jewish proverb says, "Hope is born in the very depths of despair."[1] Even as Israel was being crushed under the bondage of Egypt, God revealed His name out of the burning bush. That tragic day in September, I came to *know* God's name in a time of great despair. My tears of joy were mixed with tears of sorrow.

[1] See *Vikuach Ha-Ramban* interpreting *Lamentations Rabbah* 1:51 and *The Disputation*, directed by Geoffrey Sax, 1986.

Chapter 7:

Breaking the Silence

The artificial hill of Lachish rose suddenly out of the rolling terrain of the Judean lowlands. Carpeted with brown thorn bushes and withering thistles, the hill stood in sharp contrast to the neat green rows of grapevines and pomegranate trees stretched out in the plain below. The desolation was occasionally punctuated by a mound of earth or a collapsing stone wall. This was all that remained of what was once the second largest city in the Kingdom of Judah.

I came to Lachish in pursuit of an ancient Hebrew document unearthed in the ruins of the city gate. It was a letter scribbled on a broken piece of pottery by a Judean military commander in the final days before Judah fell to the Babylonians. I was looking for evidence that the ancient Israelites spoke God's holy name, the name God commanded the *kohanim* to speak over the people in the Priestly Blessing. I thought what better place to start than Nebuchadnezzar's invasion of 586 BCE, which culminated in the destruction of the First Temple. That devastating event was ancient Israel's very own 9/11, an event that changed God's people forever.

As I sat in the city gate, reading the history of Lachish, I could almost hear the Babylonian siege engines pounding against the city walls. In one of his prophecies, Jeremiah mentioned Lachish and the nearby Azekah as the last two fortified cities of Judah to hold out against the Babylonian army on its way to Jerusalem. The letter I had come to study was one of twenty-two documents surviving from these dark days. Most of them were communiqués written by a field commander named Hoshayahu to the governor of Lachish.

In one of these letters, Hoshayahu defended his honor after he was accused of being illiterate. Apparently, Hoshayahu was not following orders and the governor said something like, "What's the matter, can't you read?" In Hoshayahu's impassioned response, he wrote:

> Concerning that which my lord said, "You do not know how to read letters," as-Yehovah-lives, no man has ever tried to read a letter to me and indeed I read every letter that comes to me and I furthermore pay attention to it.[1]

The thing that struck me about this was the phrase "as Yehovah lives." I knew this phrase always appeared in the Hebrew Bible introducing a vow.[2] It was the ancient Hebrew way of saying, "I swear by the life of Yehovah." In Hebrew, this vow-formula consists of two words. The first is *Chay* (rhymes with "high"), meaning "life." The second is God's holy name. Hoshayahu was swearing by the life of Yehovah that he was not illiterate. Here's the really exciting thing: Hoshayahu wrote out these two Hebrew words as a single word. He was a simple man and wrote the way he spoke, blending "Chay" and "Yehovah" into one word: "Chay-Ho-Vah." In English, we do this sort of thing all the time. We call it a "contraction." However, ancient Hebrew didn't have contractions, or at least it wasn't supposed to. Writing out Chayhovah as one word would be similar to Americans who say and write, "ain't." The governor of Lachish must have fallen over laughing when he read the ancient Hebrew equivalent of, "I swear to God, I ain't illiterate!"

I almost fell over myself when I realized the significance of this. Hoshayahu's letter proved beyond any doubt that in the final days of the Kingdom of Judah, the Jews spoke God's holy name. This wasn't limited to sages teaching it to their disciples as a secret or priests in the Temple muttering it under their breath. Here was a simple soldier stationed at a minor observation post in the Judean lowlands, swearing in the eternal name of God.

---

[1] My translation of Shmuel Ahituv, *Handbook of Ancient Hebrew Inscriptions*, Jerusalem 1992 [Hebrew], pages 36–41.

[2] The vow formula "as Yehovah lives" appears forty-four times in the Hebrew Bible. God Himself swears "as I live" another twenty-three times.

By swearing in God's holy name, Hoshayahu was fulfilling both a Torah commandment and a Biblical prophecy. The Book of Deuteronomy says:

> You shall worship Yehovah… and in His name shall you swear.[1]

This commandment appears twice, almost word for word. Hoshayahu was simply doing what God commanded, swearing in God's holy name.

Not all the Israelites were as righteous as this semi-literate field commander from Lachish. The prophet Jeremiah mentions that some of the Israelites of his day swore in the name of the chief Canaanite deity: "As Baal lives." What's amazing about this particular prophecy is that it's not really about the Israelites. It is a prophecy speaking to the Gentiles about their connection to God's holy name:

> Thus says Yehovah concerning all My evil neighbors who touch the inheritance that I gave to My people Israel… it shall come to pass if they nevertheless learn the way of My people to swear in My name "As Yehovah lives," in the way that they taught My people to swear by Baal, then they shall be built in the midst of My people.[2]

When I read this prophecy, I had a terrible sensation, the type I had in nightmares when suddenly finding myself stark naked in the middle of high school or sitting down unprepared for a test. Here was an awesome responsibility that God gave Israel, to teach the nations to swear in His name, and I was completely unprepared. I needed to start by being more like Hoshayahu, that simple Israelite with a simple faith who spoke God's holy name the best he knew how, improper contraction and all.

If a lowly field officer like Hoshayahu was still speaking God's name in 586 BCE, shortly before the destruction of the First Temple, it must not have become a secret until later. I thought back to the story of Rabbi Tarfon that I encountered years earlier. Rabbi Tarfon

---

[1] Deuteronomy 6:13; 10:20.

[2] Jeremiah 12:14, 16.

was the *kohen* who performed the Priestly Blessing in the Second Temple, shortly before the Romans destroyed it in 70 CE. He reported that he heard the high priest mumbling "the name" under his breath. Some historians use the story of Rabbi Tarfon as proof that by the 1st Century CE God's name was no longer spoken in public. This has even penetrated into popular culture in the classic Monty Python movie *The Life of Brian.* In one scene, a crowd of angry villagers drags a scrawny old man dressed in nothing but a loincloth into the public square. John Cleese, in the role of the high priest, stands before the crowd, who is itching to stone the old man. He proclaims the sentence:

> Matthias, son of Deuteronomy of Gath… You have been found guilty by the elders of the town of uttering the name of our Lord. And so as a *blasphemer…* you are to be stoned to death![1]

When John Cleese says the word "blasphemer," spittle flies from his mouth and veins pop out of his forehead and neck. The crowd murmurs in collective disgust. Matthias, clad in his loincloth, can't understand what all the fuss is about. He turns to the high priest and protests incredulously:

> Look, I'd had a lovely supper, and all I said to my wife was, "That piece of halibut was good enough for Jehovah!"

The crowd gasps in horror when they hear Matthias utter the name "Jehovah" and the high priest points an accusing finger, "Blasphemy! He said it again!" I had to agree with Matthias, son of Deuteronomy of Gath. If the Bible didn't forbid uttering the name of God, then who were the high priest and the town elders to condemn him for it?

Monty Python notwithstanding, I still wondered whether uttering God's name really was considered "blasphemy" in the 1st Century CE. I decided to go back to the Talmudic report of Rabbi Tarfon and look at it more closely. What I found came as a complete surprise. The section in the Talmud that introduced this story begins:

---

[1] *Life of Brian*, directed by Terry Jones, 1979.

> Our rabbis taught: At first, they used to transmit *the twelve-letter name* to every man. Ever since the indiscreet multiplied, they would [only] transmit it to the discreet priests and the discreet priests swallow it during the chanting of their brother priests.[1]

What immediately follows is the story of Rabbi Tarfon ascending the platform in the Temple to pronounce the Priestly Blessing and hearing the high priest "swallowing the Name during the chanting of his brother priests." Taken in context, Rabbi Tarfon was not speaking about the Tetragrammaton. He was talking about a different name, a twelve-letter name, a name so secret no one even knows what the consonants are. Since the twelve-letter name of God is not mentioned anywhere in the Bible I was fine leaving it a secret. The name that God revealed to Moses and commanded him to proclaim to the Israelites, the name he called "My name forever," is the four-letter name YHVH, vocalized in the Aleppo Codex and Leningrad Codex as "Yehovah."

All of this brought me back once again to the closing words of the Priestly Blessing in the Book of Numbers: "And they shall place My name on the children of Israel and I will bless them."[2] Even the rabbis admitted that placing the name on Israel, speaking the actual name of God over the people, was an integral part of the Priestly Blessing in the Temple. While the high priest was mumbling the twelve-letter name under his breath, the other Temple priests must have been chanting the Tetragrammaton, the four-letter name, for the Jewish multitudes to hear. The name Yehovah could hardly have been a secret if the Temple priests were chanting it every day in the Temple, three times, once in each line of the Priestly Blessing.

As I delved deeper into the history, I discovered that the Priestly Blessing was not the only time the Jewish multitudes heard the Tetragrammaton in the Temple. The high priest used to pronounce it ten times during the annual service for Yom Kippur, the Day of Atonement. I remember being taught this as a child but always

---

[1] *Babylonian Talmud*, Kidushin 71a.

[2] Numbers 6:27.

thought this was something the high priest did in the secrecy of the holy of holies. However, the Mishnah describes how this ceremony was performed in the final decades of the Second Temple:

> When the multitudes standing in the courtyard heard the Tetragrammaton (*Shem HaMeforash*) come forth from the mouth of the high priest, they would kneel, prostrate, and fall on their faces, and then say, "Blessed is the glorious name of His kingdom forever."[1]

This ritual was repeated ten times every Yom Kippur, once for each time the high priest pronounced the name during the sacrificial service. As I was reading about this ritual, I suddenly realized I had rehearsed this ceremony myself as a young boy in the synagogue. Every year on Yom Kippur, I remember my father rushing me out of the synagogue prayer hall in the middle of the service so we could wash our hands. He would then take a stack of paper towels and lay them out on the floor of the main prayer hall.[2] When the cantor recited certain words, we would kneel down on the paper towels and press our hands and heads to the ground, the way Muslims do when they pray. My father explained to me that this commemorated a ritual of our ancestors in the Jerusalem Temple. I had no idea at the time that it had anything to do with God's name.[3] Now I realized that as long as the Temple stood, God's name could not have been a secret. The Jewish multitudes heard it ten times every Yom Kippur directly from the mouth of the high priest. They also heard it three times every day from the regular priests pronouncing the Priestly Blessing. If this was a secret, it was the worst kept secret in history.

The Temple priests were not the only ones to speak God's holy name. The Book of Chronicles describes a celebration that took place in Jerusalem at the time of King David, a time when there was

---

[1] *Mishnah*, Yoma 6:2.

[2] The purpose of the paper towels was to avoid prostrating directly on the floor, which according to Talmudic law is only permissible in the Jerusalem Temple (*Babylonian Talmud*, Megillah 25a).

[3] This ritual is repeated every Yom Kippur in Orthodox Jewish synagogues throughout the world.

no Temple. The celebration began with the Levites issuing a call to praise God's name:

> Praise Yehovah; call on His name; proclaim His deeds among the peoples.[1]

These were not mere ceremonial words. After the Levites finished singing, the Jewish multitudes responded to their call to praise God's name:

> ...and all the people said, "Amen and praise Yehovah."[2]

I thought about how far we had come from the time when all of Israel proclaimed and praised God's name. Today, His eternal name has become a secret, banned from the synagogues, relegated to the dusty pages of history. I hate secrets and decided I needed to honor God's name by shattering the conspiracy of silence. I had that feeling again, the one of finding myself in a dream naked in the middle of high school, that sense of unpreparedness. I was not a public speaker at the time and did not know how to go about doing this. The words of Moses echoed in my head, "Please, O Lord, I have never been a man of words, either in times past or now that You have spoken to Your servant; I am slow of speech and slow of tongue."[3] I had no idea how I was going to respond to the call of the Levites and publicly proclaim and praise God's holy name.

My friend, Keith Johnson, likes to say, "When God provides vision, He always provides provision." This certainly was true in my case. I have been blessed with many unexpected opportunities to teach the Word of God and to proclaim His name. When I started out, I fumbled my words worse than Moses, but over the years, God has given me the ability and wisdom to do honor to His name. Despite all this, I never intended to put the focus of my teaching on God's name until several years ago when Keith and I went on a speaking tour together. Little did I know our joint book about a

---

[1] 1 Chronicles 16:8.
[2] 1 Chronicles 16:36.
[3] Exodus 4:10 [NJPS].

Christian prayer would lead me to proclaim God's holy name around the world and ultimately in a Jewish synagogue.

The catalyst for this was something that happened after one of our speaking events, at the home of an old man who was hosting us. That night Keith taught the predominately Christian audience that "the Father" has a name and that name is "Yehovah." A few hours after the event, Keith was sitting in the old man's living room speaking to him about the name. The old man told Keith he had been a Christian all his life and "never knew the Father's name." In recent years, the old man started exploring the Hebrew roots of Christianity. He realized Jesus lived as a Jew and wanted to emulate his "Messiah" by also living as a Jew. He joined a "Messianic" congregation to connect more with the faith of Jesus. He would go to his congregation every Saturday, dress up in traditional Jewish garb, and recite traditional Jewish prayers. The octogenarian even went through a Bar Mitzvah, a rite-of-passage for Jewish boys when they turn thirteen.

One of the things they told the old man at his Messianic congregation was never to utter the name "Jesus." They taught him that he must always call Jesus by his original Hebrew name, "Yeshua." One day it occurred to the old man that "if the name of the Son is Yeshua, then maybe the Father also has a name." He asked his congregation leaders about this, and they told him that "the Father's name" was too holy for him to know and too sacred for him to pronounce.

"They told me I don't need to know that name," the old man concluded his testimony.

Keith responded by telling the old man that the name of Yehovah appears nearly 7,000 times in the Hebrew Bible and then finally said, "I wish I could show you the name in my Bible."

The old man repeated once again, "They told me I don't need to know that name."

I was sitting in the dining room, about ten feet away, munching on a bowl of Shredded Wheat and getting a little annoyed as Keith and the old man went back and forth. Keith kept saying he wanted to show the old man the name in his Bible, and the old man kept parroting the same refrain, "They told me I don't need to know that name."

As I reached the bottom of my bowl of late-night cereal, I decided to offer some sagely advice that would put a quick end to the verbal stalemate. "Do it, Keith! Go get your Hebrew Bible and show it to him!" I interjected.

When I said this, the old man got up and was about to storm out of his own living room. I could see the fear in his eyes, the fear of confronting God's eternal name. Seeing this broke my heart and made me think of the words of the prophet Isaiah who said:

> Also the sons of the foreigner who join themselves to Yehovah, to serve Him, *and to love the name of Yehovah…* Even them I will bring to My holy mountain, and make them joyful in My house of prayer… for My house shall be called a house of prayer for all nations.[1]

The promise at the end of this passage is one of the most famous in the entire Bible: God's house will be called "a house of prayer for all nations." An integral part of this promise is that the foreigners who join themselves to the one true God will "love the name of Yehovah." How sad, I thought, that this old man wanted to be close to God, had asked about His eternal name, but was taught to stay far away from it and even to fear it. That night, in the old man's dining room, I made the decision to speak about God's name everywhere I was invited to teach on the Hebrew origins of the "Lord's Prayer."

The last place I ever expected to speak on this topic was a Jewish synagogue. However, Keith's words proved true: *when God provides vision, He always provides provision.* The provision came on a warm spring afternoon in Manhattan at a Starbucks on the corner of 87th and Lexington. I was sitting there with a Venti nonfat latte trying to memorize a sixty-second speech. I've never memorized a speech in my life. At countless venues, I always just got up and spoke what was on my mind. This was different. It was the Jewish Book Council, the Jewish publishing world's version of speed-dating. Two hundred

---

[1] Isaiah 56:6–7.

fifty authors got two minutes each to pitch their books to representatives of one hundred Jewish organizations. The coveted prize? An invitation to speak at a synagogue or Jewish Community Center as part of the Jewish Book Network.

When I sent in the application for *A Prayer to Our Father,* I assumed it would be turned down. But it wasn't. So here we are, at Starbucks, just hours away from the event. What was I thinking, coming here with an African American Methodist pastor to pitch a book on the Hebrew origins of a *Christian* prayer to the *Jewish* Book Council? And in only two minutes! It usually takes me forty-five minutes just to say my name. And I have to split my two minutes with Keith, so all I really have is sixty seconds. Every word has to be chosen strategically for maximum effect. Every word has to be carefully sifted and crafted to intrigue but to not offend. Every word needs to be right. We won't get any invitations anyway, but maybe, just maybe, some of the representatives will read the complimentary copies of the book we submitted as part of the application process.

I need more latte! Sip coffee. Deep breath. *Ok, I'll just keep repeating the speech to Keith until I get it right.* I'm half way through my tenth repetition when a gorgeous woman in a classy Manhattan suit jaywalks across 87th Street.

Keith follows my fixed gaze until he spots the young lady and bursts out laughing, "Nehemia, you need to concentrate!"

Two hours later, we are in the basement of the Park Avenue Synagogue in Manhattan, waiting for the event to begin. I am talking to a famous Jewish author who has just come out with his third popular book on Kabbalah. He tells me that this is the first time he has been to the Jewish Book Council. Most of the two hundred fifty authors won't get a single invite, he explains, but just to be here is an honor.

Keith turns to me with a panicked look, "Nehemia, what are we doing here?"

The event is about to begin. The organizer explains to us the procedure. Each speaker will get exactly two minutes. She'll warn the speaker when he has fifteen seconds left. When his time is up, she'll signal him. If he goes fifteen seconds over, she'll get up and kick him off the podium. The next speaker needs to be waiting in a hot seat to switch out the last one as soon as he finishes. This isn't "Israeli time." Two minutes really means two minutes.

The event finally begins. It is going like clockwork. As the other authors pitch their books, I am flipping through the catalogue. I see there are many books on the Holocaust, Middle-East politics, cookbooks, and sundry topics. But nothing on interfaith dialogue or the Jewish roots of Christianity. There's only one book like that. Our book. Gulp. Deep breaths. Keith is sitting next to me with his arms folded across his chest, trying to suppress a laugh. Usually he's the nervous one, and I'm calm. Ok, we're up next. I know my speech. I memorized all sixty seconds and know every word I need to say.

I walk up to the podium with Keith trailing behind me. I go first. I look out across the room at hundreds of Jewish faces. There is complete silence as they are waiting for me to speak. Time stands still. *Nothing! I can't remember what I'm supposed to say! Ok, I'm just going to say what's on my mind.* I tell it to them straight. I don't remember exactly what I said but it went something like this:

> You're probably wondering, what on earth an Israeli Bible scholar and an African American Methodist pastor are doing at the Jewish Book Council speaking about the Hebrew origins of what his people—motioning to Keith—call the "Lord's Prayer." Well, Jesus was a Jew and he taught this prayer to the Jewish multitudes in Israel. That means the most famous Christian prayer is actually a prayer of Jewish origin. This prayer can't be fully understood without first understanding its Jewish background and context. This isn't a new discovery. Over thirty years ago, a rabbi at the Jewish Theological Seminary wrote a book about the Jewish background of the Lord's Prayer. What we've done is taken it one step further and used the study of the Jewish and Hebrew background of the most beloved prayer in the Christian world as the basis for interfaith dialogue.

That was less than sixty seconds but I don't know what else to say. I slide over to the side of the podium so Keith can speak.

He starts off in Hebrew, "Shalom friends. My name is Keith Johnson."

I interject in Hebrew, "Hey, speak English!" The crowd roars with laughter. Keith then does the rest of his *spiel* in English. He hits it out of the park as usual. That was a long two minutes.

The next morning Keith and I part ways. He returns to Charlotte, and I spend the day in New York waiting for my flight back to Israel. Weeks go by, and we don't hear anything. I am sure we won't get any invites. The author of the books on Kabbalah e-mails me, saying that I shouldn't feel bad because he didn't get any invites either. Still, it wasn't a total loss. Hopefully, someone was inspired to read the book. Then the invites arrive. We end up with four of them. They are all for November during Jewish Book Month. The Karaite Bible scholar and the African-American Methodist pastor are set to participate in the Jewish Book Network speaking tour during Jewish Book Month, and that's not the punch line of a joke.

This is how I ended up teaching on the Hebrew origins of the "Lord's Prayer" at a Reform Jewish synagogue in the Deep South. At the synagogue, I shared about the section in the prayer that says, "hallowed be thy name." I explained that in both Hebrew and Greek it says, "may Your name be sanctified," which grammatically is a call to action to sanctify God's name.[1] The prayer starts out "Our Father in heaven" so it must be talking about the name of our heavenly Father, which both Jews and Christians are in full agreement on. What I think is so amazing about this, I explain, is that most Christians pray either directly to Jesus or "in Jesus' name." As a Jew, I'm not comfortable participating in a prayer like that. When I say this, the heads across the room nod in agreement, and I hear a chorus of muffled "mhmms."

After a brief pause I continue. Jesus taught the Jewish multitudes to pray to "Our Father in heaven." He did not tell them to sanctify his own name but rather to sanctify our heavenly Father's name. This begs the question: What is the name of our heavenly Father? I then

---

[1] Matthew 6:9 and see *A Prayer to Our Father*, pages 97–113.

explain that Moses asked the same question, and God gave His famous answer in the 3rd chapter of Exodus. At this point in the presentation, I'm supposed to tell the audience what that name is, the eternal name that God revealed to Moses. The name He commanded the *kohanim* to proclaim over the people in the Priestly Blessing. The name about which God said, "this is My name forever, this is My memorial for every generation."[1] But I am speaking at a Jewish synagogue as a guest and I want to be respectful. I turn to the cantor who is leading the congregation today and ask if it would be offensive for me to speak the name. He tells me to go right ahead, that it's not a problem whatsoever. Being raised Orthodox with rabbinical tradition forbidding me to utter God's holy name, I am taken a little by surprise. I had come to the synagogue expecting to talk about the name but not actually proclaim it. While I am zealous about God's holy name, I also have good manners and common decency. I would not enter as a guest into someone else's house of worship and do something that I know offends them. However, the cantor said it was all right.

I stand there in the synagogue and hold my breath as I am about to proclaim the name. For a moment, there is complete silence, a moment that seems to last forever. Over the silence, I could have sworn I heard John Cleese in his role as high priest, pointing an accusing finger at me, and shouting in his posh British accent, "Blasphemy!"

I close my eyes to brace for the impact of the stones, but none arrive. When I open my eyes, John Cleese is gone. All I see is the welcoming smile of the cantor and the audience looking to me with anticipation to hear God's eternal name. As the name "Yehovah" comes forth from my lips, I feel a great sense of relief. A pressure building up inside for years is finally released. God's name resonates across the prayer hall of the synagogue. I am living the words of the Psalmist:

---

[1] Exodus 3:15.

I will declare Your name to my brethren; in the midst of the assembly, I will praise You.[1]

[1] Psalms 22:22[23] [NKJV].

Chapter 8:

Live Long and Prosper

The gaunt Galilean preacher drags a large wooden beam down the center of the narrow village street. One end of the beam weighs heavily on his right shoulder causing him to hunch over. The other end scrapes along the ground, cutting its way through filth. The preacher's left eye is swollen shut from an earlier beating. Villagers line the street, some shouting curses at the preacher, others weeping over his plight. A Roman soldier steps out of the crowd, swinging a whip through the air. The whip cracks as it breaks the sound barrier, sending a small startled dog fleeing down a side-alley. The whip comes down hard on the preacher's back, spraying bystanders with droplets of blood. A passerby is pressed into service to help carry the heavy beam. When they reach the top of the hill just outside the village, the preacher collapses. Two Roman soldiers secure him to the wooden beam as a satisfied centurion looks on. The soldiers plant one end of the beam in a small hole hewn in the rock and raise the other end with ropes. Today's execution is a rabbi. His name: Hanina ben Teradion. The method of execution: burning at the stake. The crime: speaking the name of the Jewish God in public.

When I came across the story of Rabbi Hanina ben Teradion, I couldn't believe it. The Talmud relates that the Romans executed this rabbi sometime between 130 and 138 CE during the reign of the emperor Hadrian, who issued a series of decrees designed to eradicate the Jewish faith. Rabbi Hanina was martyred during these persecutions after speaking the name of God in public, as the Talmud reports:

> The [Romans] brought forth Rabbi Hanina ben Teradion and asked him, "Why did you engage in the study of the Torah?" He answered, "Because the Lord my God commanded me." They immediately sentenced him to be

> burned… They sentenced him to be burned because he used to pronounce the name the way it is written…[1]

The Romans executed Rabbi Hanina for publicly teaching the Torah. During his illegal lessons, Rabbi Hanina "used to pronounce the name the way it is written." This transgression earned him a particularly vicious mode of execution, as the Talmud further relates:

> They took hold of him, wrapped him in a Torah Scroll, surrounded him in bundles of branches and set them on fire. They also brought tufts of wool, which they had soaked in water, and placed them over his heart, so that he should not expire quickly.[2]

The story of Rabbi Hanina puzzled later rabbis. By the 3rd Century, the pronunciation of God's name had become a secret and they couldn't understand why this martyred rabbi would speak it publicly a hundred years earlier. They believed it acceptable for Rabbi Hanina to speak God's name in the secrecy of a private Torah teaching but not in a public lesson. According to these later rabbis, it was God who was offended by this and who sentenced Rabbi Hanina to be burned alive at the hand of the Romans.[3]

This later rabbinical explanation notwithstanding, there was no disputing that Rabbi Hanina "used to pronounce the name the way it is written," meaning he spoke the name of Yehovah in public on multiple occasions. Another rabbinical source corroborated that it was commonplace in the period of the Hadrianic persecutions for Jews to pronounce the Tetragrammaton.[4] Evidently, the Romans wanted to put a stop to this, so they made an example of Rabbi Hanina.

I was a little confused why the Romans would care about a Jew speaking God's holy name until I came across an early rabbinical report about the Greek persecutions during the time of the Maccabees, three hundred years before Hadrian:

---

[1] *Babylonian Talmud*, Avodah Zarah 17b–18a.
[2] *Babylonian Talmud*, Avodah Zarah 18a.
[3] *Babylonian Talmud*, Avodah Zarah 18a.
[4] *Midrash Psalms* on Psalms 36:7[8].

> The Greeks made decrees to eradicate Israel, ordering them to deny the kingdom of heaven, to declare that they have no portion with the God of Israel, *and not to mention the heavenly name on their lips.*[1]

I knew Hadrian patterned his anti-Jewish decrees after those of the Greeks and he must have also banned speaking God's heavenly name as the Greeks did.

I was shocked to learn that the ban on speaking God's name started out as a Roman decree. I needed to know when the rabbis adopted this Roman ban and why. I eventually discovered that the earliest rabbinical teaching against speaking God's name dated to shortly after Rabbi Hanina's martyrdom. This new ruling appeared in the name of Abba Saul, one of the rabbis to survive the Hadrianic persecutions.[2] I couldn't believe this was a coincidence. Here, I have to humble myself as a Karaite Jew and give credit to the rabbis for something they brilliantly accomplished. One of the ways the rabbis preserved the Jewish people during millennia of persecution was by adapting to the changing circumstances of foreign occupation and dispersion. This is a survival strategy I have mixed feelings about, but I can't deny it worked.

An early example of this strategy is the teaching that a rabbinical court should never impose the death penalty more than once in seventy years.[3] This teaching was supported by a series of interpretations that made it virtually impossible to sentence someone to death in a rabbinical court. These rulings coincided with the Roman subjugation of Judea, which stripped the rabbis of the authority to carry out the death penalty.[4] Other famous examples are the Calendar Reform of Hillel II in 359 CE and the "Takanot of Rabbenu Gershom" in the 10th Century, both of which adapted rabbinical law to the limitations imposed by despotic foreign rule.

---

[1] *Scholion on Megilat Ta'anit*, 3rd of Tishrei.
[2] *Mishnah*, Sanhedrin 10:1.
[3] *Mishnah*, Makkot 1:10.
[4] *Ethics of the Fathers*, 1:9; *Mishnah*, Makkot 1:10.

The rabbinical ban on using God's name in public may have been a similar adaptation. After the martyrdom of Rabbi Hanina, the rabbis had to make a choice between losing an entire generation of Jewish leaders or adapting to the Roman prohibition against speaking God's name. In private, the rabbis continued to "transmit the four-letter name to their disciples once in a seven-year period."[1] However, in public, in earshot of Roman collaborators, they replaced God's name with Adonai (Lord).

The ban on the name put the *kohanim*, the Aaronic priests, in a difficult position. God commanded them to place His holy name over the people during the Priestly Blessing, but the rabbis forbade them to speak it. They eventually found an ingenious workaround through a unique hand gesture they made when reciting the blessing. It was the same hand gesture Mr. Spock used to make in the old *Star Trek* series—but with *both* hands. This was more than a coincidence. The actor who played Spock was a Jew who saw the *kohanim* display this in the synagogue as a child. He even combined it with his own Vulcan version of the Priestly Blessing: "Live long and prosper!"[2] I chuckled when I thought about this. In the most abstract terms, this really was the basic message of the ancient Hebrew blessing from the Book of Numbers, long life and prosperity.

What the Jewish actor who played Spock didn't know was that his character was proclaiming the holy name of Yehovah all over the universe through this Vulcan greeting. The idiosyncratic way of holding the hands he saw in the synagogue was actually a cipher for God's holy name. One of the earliest sources to mention it explains, "the priest would form the letters of the Tetragrammaton with his hands."[3]

When I first read this, I thought it was farfetched until I found a diagram of the way the *kohanim* hold their hands during the Priestly Blessing in an old Hebrew book. It had two of the letters of God's holy name inscribed on each of the wrists, and I could see how the strange way of holding the fingers corresponded to the letters of the

[1] *Babylonian Talmud*, Kidushin 71a.
[2] *Star Trek*, created by Gene Roddenberry, 1966–1969.
[3] Bachya ben Asher, *Biur Al Ha-Torah*, volume 3, page 34.

Tetragrammaton. It formed the letters Yod-Hay-Vav-Hay about as well as the modern "OK" hand gesture forms the letter "K." If you didn't know what it was supposed to mean, you'd never figure it out. Of course, that was exactly the point. Using this cryptic sign language allowed the Aaronic priests to place God's name on the people despite the rabbinical prohibition to speak it.[1]

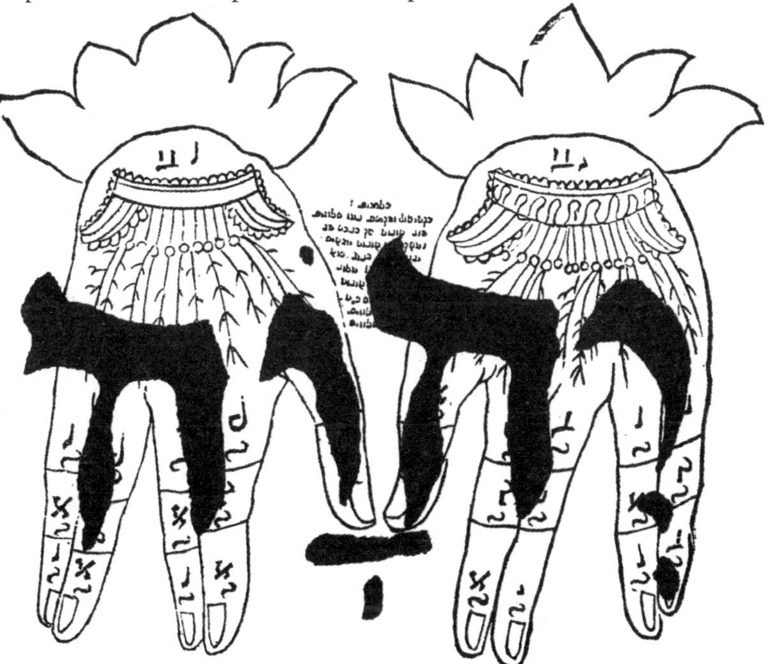

When I discovered that the rabbinical ban on God's holy name was instituted as a protective measure against Roman persecution, I felt like I uncovered a great secret that I needed to share. I decided to approach a young rabbi I knew and hear his opinion. I met him at his synagogue in Jerusalem and started to tell him about the Romans executing Hanina ben Teradion for speaking God's name. He stopped me midway through and told me he knew all about it. I then told him about finding the name of God with a full set of vowels in the Aleppo Codex.

[1] Shabbathai Horowitz, *Shefa Tal*, Hanau 1612, page 15. I superimposed the letters and vowels of the Tetragrammaton from the Aleppo Codex to show how this hand gesture forms the name.

"The true pronunciation of God's name is Yehovah!" I announced excitedly.

The rabbi leaned back in his chair and responded with a single word: "*Peshita.*" In Aramaic this literally means "simple," but in Talmudic jargon it is a sarcastic way of saying, "Obviously, Sherlock." After a long awkward pause, he asked me never to speak the Almighty's holy name in his presence again.

"Men greater than either of us established the tradition of not speaking Hashem's name," he told me assuredly, "and only men greater than us can change it back."

I was amazed at how profoundly the rabbi epitomized the difference between a rabbinical and a Karaite worldview. He did not dispute the Scriptural or historical facts but deferred to the authority of the rabbinical sages. From my perspective, this was not about authority; it was about truth. When I shared this thought with him, he snapped back that I was being extremely arrogant. I chuckled when he said this and nodded my head in agreement. I suppose he was right, in a way. It was a little arrogant of me thinking I could decide for myself how to live by Scripture even when it ran contrary to generations of Jewish tradition.

I think this attitude stems from my experiences as a child studying the teachings of the ancient rabbis. I would read things in their writings that seemed completely ludicrous to me. When I brought them up to my teachers, I was told not to worry about it, that if these ancient rabbis were wrong they would bear the blame. It was not for me to judge whether these great sages were right or wrong; it was simply my duty to submit to their authority and obey. That didn't make any sense to me.

One day, one of my rabbis got very upset with me for constantly disagreeing with the interpretations of the Talmudic sages and bellowed at the top of his lungs, "Who are you to question all these great learned men?"

I was only ten years old at the time, but I was full of conviction. "Who am I?" I thought, "I'm the one who has to stand before God on the Day of Judgment and answer for my actions." The way I saw it this made me the most important person in the world when it came to deciding how *I* was going to live *my* life. As long as I could tell God I was following the words of His prophets, I didn't mind being at odds with generations of learned rabbis.

As these thoughts raced through my mind, the words of the young rabbi hung in the air like one of those cartoon balloons. He had said "only men greater than us can change it back." When the dime finally dropped, the gravity of his statement struck me.

"What do you mean *change it back*?" I asked him in surprise.

He smiled, sat up in his chair, and began to tell me how the ancient rabbis—the ones I thought I knew better than—never intended the tradition of substituting God's name with Adonai (Lord) to be permanent.

"As soon as the Mashiach (Messiah) comes," he explained, "we will go back to speaking Hashem's name."

He pulled a large dusty volume off his shelf and opened up to a passage in the Talmud that quoted a 4th Century rabbi:

> This world is not like the world to come. In this world, the name is written Yeho[vah] and read Ado[nai] but in the world to come it *will be one*, written Yeho[vah] and read Yeho[vah].[1]

"The world to come in the writings of our sages," he explained, "refers to the earthly kingdom of the Mashiach."

He said that in the kingdom of the Messiah, God's name will no longer be a secret and will be spoken the way it is written. The young rabbi didn't stop there. He told me the ancient sages knew it would not only be Israel speaking God's name. When they said God's name "will be one" in the world to come they were basing themselves on a verse in the Book of Zechariah, which prophesied:

> Yehovah shall be king over the entire earth and on that day Yehovah will be one and His name will be one.[2]

I immediately recognized this as the closing line of traditional daily prayers and one I recited every day growing up as an Orthodox

---

[1] *Babylonian Talmud*, Pesachim 50a.
[2] Zechariah 14:9.

Jew. I have to confess that I was not the best Orthodox Jew. My heart was never really in it. It would be an understatement to say I occasionally arrived late for prayers. But I almost always made it by the end of the service. I remember loving this verse and not only because it meant that the boring prayer service was about to be over. The prophecy that God would be "king over the entire earth" excited me every morning with the promise of a future of world peace under the kingship of the one true God. As a young man, I focused on that future kingdom and didn't give much thought to the part about God's name. Now I could see the verse was also saying in that future of world peace, all mankind would call God by the same name, His eternal name, the name Yehovah.

Some of my Christian friends speak in fear and trepidation of the impending "one-world government" that will engulf all of humanity. Personally, I look forward to the one-world government under the kingship of the one true God, with the King Messiah, His flesh and blood representative on earth, as promised through the prophet Ezekiel:

> And I Yehovah will be their God, and My servant David a prince among them; I Yehovah have spoken it.[1]

In this future era of world peace, every human being will call upon the name of Yehovah and serve Him with one accord, standing shoulder-to-shoulder to build up His name. I was becoming increasingly convinced that the secret of God's name needed to end now. When the Messiah comes to reign as a flesh and blood king on the throne of David, I don't want to have to tell him, "I was waiting for you to confess God's name, to pray in His name, and to praise His name." I'd rather be able to tell him I did the best I could to live by the Word of God while I was waiting for His earthly kingdom.

The Romans are gone and the Hadrianic persecutions a distant memory. So why do the Jewish People continue to observe something that lost its relevance over a thousand years ago? Tevye

---

[1] Ezekiel 37:24

said it best in *Fiddler on the Roof*, "Tradition! Tradition!"[1] Once a practice gets entrenched and becomes tradition, it is hard to dislodge it, even when it loses its original relevance.

Tradition isn't all bad. It can provide people with a sense of stability, as Tevye so wisely said, "because of our traditions we've kept our balance for many, many years." The name of the musical *Fiddler on the Roof* is itself a metaphor for the instability brought about by casting off the chains of tradition. Early in the film Tevye explains, "without our traditions, our lives would be as shaky as a fiddler on the roof." The camera immediately cuts to a fiddler precariously balanced on a rooftop.

Where tradition becomes a problem is when it gets confused with Scripture. Tevye was constantly justifying his traditions with the words, "as the good book says." He was so immersed in tradition he had no idea where it ended and Scripture began. He naively believed that "because of our traditions, every one of us knows… what God expects him to do."

The way I see it, this is precisely the wrong approach to take. Tradition is what *men* expect us to do, not what God expects of us. God expects us to show our love for Him by keeping *His* commandments, not by following our own man-made traditions. Confusing tradition with the commandments of God turns it into what the prophet Isaiah called "a commandment of men learned by rote."[2]

I have to admit that this is a very Karaite attitude towards tradition. The Karaite walk of faith, free from the bonds of tradition, is extremely liberating but can also be a bit scary. A famous rabbi once compared being a Karaite, not guided by tradition, to wandering through a desert, never knowing what will be around the next corner. There is some truth to this. The Karaite journey requires the faith of Abraham who left the land of his forefathers. Abraham set out on a journey through the desert with no idea where he was going or when he would get there. He had no map. No GPS. He was

---

[1] *Fiddler on the Roof*, directed by Norman Jewison, 1971.

[2] Isaiah 29:13 [NJPS] and see my book *The Hebrew Yeshua vs. the Greek Jesus*, Hilkiah Press 2005, pages 23–24.

following God's voice obediently. Living as a Karaite requires this sort of obedience and faith, allowing God's words in the Hebrew Bible to be your guide.

I understood why the Orthodox rabbis maintained the ban on speaking God's eternal name. Their devotion to the authority of tradition outlived the original purpose of the ban. However, the last place I expected tradition to rear its ugly little head was among my own Karaite brothers. The word "Karaite" means "Scripturalist" and the name implies that Karaite Jews are guided by Scripture and not by tradition. No Scriptural reason to refrain from speaking God's name exists, so I assumed my fellow Karaites would jump on board and proclaim God's holy name from every rooftop. Unfortunately, not every Karaite lives up to the Scripturalist ideal, at least as I understand it. I was presented with three arguments against speaking God's name, each from different Karaites with varying levels of commitment to following Scripture over tradition.

I encountered the first objection when I eagerly shared what I learned about the name with an old Karaite "rabbi" in Jerusalem. As a side note, I've always been baffled why some Karaite Jews insist on using the title "rabbi." This title implies a teacher who has God-given authority to interpret Scripture for others. The way I see it, Scripture only gives this authority to the high priest at the Temple and the Davidic Messiah who reigns as king over Israel. Today, with no high priest and no flesh and blood Davidic king, Karaite Judaism teaches that every human being is equal before God. This is the theory, in any event. In practice, I sometimes feel like one of the critters in George Orwell's *Animal Farm.* When the animals in the book overthrow their human masters, they inscribe their main guiding principle on the barn wall: "All animals are equal." Over time, the pigs take over the farm and change this to, "All animals are equal, but some animals are more equal than others."[1] I sometimes wonder if the guiding principle of some Karaite *rabbis* isn't, "All Karaites are equal, but some Karaites are more equal than others."

---

[1] George Orwell, *Animal Farm*, 1945.

Anyway, when I approached the old Karaite "rabbi" in Jerusalem and told him that I believed we needed to go back to praying in God's holy name, he strongly objected. He explained that his family have been Karaite Jews for dozens of generations and have never been in the habit of calling upon God's name. He insisted the practice just wasn't the Karaite way. He had no problem pronouncing the name, which incidentally he knew to be "Yehovah," even before I shared this detail with him. However, regularly using God's name was simply not part of his ancient tradition of worship. I couldn't believe it. I had met the Karaite *Tevye* and could hear him singing, "Unheard of… absurd… unthinkable… tradition… tradition!"

I was disappointed by his attitude, but I decided to deal with him on his own terms. If he needed to see Karaite Jews historically speaking God's name, then I would find him some. I scoured ancient sources and discovered a 10th Century Karaite historian named Jacob Kirkisani. In a famous book on the history of Judaism, he reported that many of the Karaite Jews of his day spoke the name of God. According to Kirkisani, one faction of Karaite Jews in Persia took this to the extreme saying that anyone who replaced the name of God with *Adonai* (Lord) was an "unbeliever."[1] Not all Karaite Jews agreed with this position, but the old Karaite rabbi certainly could not claim that praying to God using His name was an "un-Karaite" thing to do.

I also pointed out to the old Karaite rabbi that the most important period of history to consider was the Scriptures themselves. The people in the Hebrew Bible freely used God's name beginning in the time of Enosh, the grandson of Adam, and all the way through the time of Ezra.[2] This included Abraham, Isaac, Jacob, Moses, David, Solomon and countless others.[3] In ancient Israel, the name of God was not only used in prayers, praises, and vows, but it

---

[1] Bruno Chiesa and Wilfrid Lockwood, *Ya'qub al-Qirqisani on Jewish Sects and Christianity*, Frankfurt 1984, page 155.

[2] Genesis 4:26; Ezra 7:27.

[3] Genesis 12:8 (Abraham); 26:25 (Isaac); 28:16 (Jacob); Exodus 5:1 (Moses); 1 Samuel 17:37 (David); 1 Kings 8:12 (Solomon).

was even used as an everyday greeting.[1] The first one known to use this greeting was the angel who approached Gideon with the words, "Yehovah be with you."[2] At this point in the story, Gideon did not know he was speaking to an angel. He thought he was speaking to a regular man, addressing him with a common greeting.

The practice of greeting people in the name of Yehovah was still in vogue over a thousand years after Gideon. The early rabbis taught, "a man is required to greet his fellow using the name."[3] This was the common Jewish greeting until the time of the ban on speaking God's name, which came in the wake of the martyrdom of Hanina ben Teradion. I thought I proved my case pretty well to the old Karaite rabbi, but he was not convinced. The power of tradition is such that Scripture and historical facts rarely sway those who are guided by it.

The second Karaite objection to speaking God's name was something I stumbled across in the writings of a Bible commentator named Daniel Kumisi. Living in the 9th Century, Kumisi is famous in Jewish history for being the first Zionist. Up until his time, Jews prayed night and day about returning to the Land of Israel but no one actually did anything about it. Kumisi formulated the first practical plan for Jews to return to Zion. He then put his money where his mouth was by making *Aliyah*—immigrating to Israel—around the year 880 CE. In one of his letters calling on the Jews of Persia to return to the Land of Israel, Kumisi also wrote about the pronunciation of God's name.

Speaking God's name appears to have been popular among Kumisi's readers in Persia, but he was vehemently opposed to it. He based his opposition on a verse in the Book of Leviticus, which the King James Version translates:

> And he that *blasphemeth* the name of the LORD shall surely be put to death.[4]

---

[1] Deuteronomy 9:26 (prayer); 2 Samuel 22:4 (praise); Judges 8:19 (vows); Ruth 2:4 (greeting).
[2] Judges 6:12.
[3] *Mishnah*, Berachot 9:5 (see also *A Prayer to Our Father*, page 106 note 24).
[4] Leviticus 24:16 [KJV].

In the original Hebrew, it doesn't say, "blasphemeth," it says:

> But he who *expressly speaks* the name of Yehovah, shall surely be put to death.[1]

Kumisi took this to be a prohibition against speaking God's name.

When I looked up the verse and read the entire passage, I couldn't help but roll my eyes. Here the context was crucial. The section in Leviticus begins with a man who "expressly spoke the name and cursed."[2] After the public execution of the offender, God revealed to Moses the laws regarding cursing God and His name:

> And to the children of Israel speak saying, "Any man who curses his God, shall bear his sin. But he who expressly speaks the name of Yehovah shall surely be put to death."[3]

According to this, if a person says, "Cursed be God," he bears his sin, meaning God will deal with him in His own time and manner. However, if he expressly speaks the name of Yehovah in his curse, an authorized court must publicly execute him. The crime of the offender earlier in the passage wasn't just cursing God but also pronouncing the Tetragrammaton in his curse, which earned him the death penalty. The context here was obviously cursing God's name, not just innocently speaking it.

While I was convinced that Kumisi was wrong on the issue of the name, I have to give him credit for something he wrote after explaining his position. It's one of the most profound things I have ever read, and I can honestly say it changed my life:

> I wrote for you my opinion concerning speaking the name of the Lord. As for you, investigate the matter according to your own wisdom lest you do according to my wisdom, relying on my opinion. For anyone who relies with blind acceptance on one of the teachers of the Exile, without

---

[1] Leviticus 24:16.

[2] Leviticus 24:11. KJV translates: "blasphemed the name of the LORD, and cursed."

[3] Leviticus 24:15–16.

> investigating well according to his own wisdom is like one engaged in idol worship.[1]

Kumisi was saying that blindly accepting what someone says in matters of faith turns that person's words into an idol. Instead of worshipping God based on what God said in Scripture, you end up worshipping God based on what men have said. Even if those men happen to be right in their understanding of Scripture, you've set them up as an intermediary between you and God. That's exactly what an idol is, an intermediary that people worship instead of directly worshipping God.

What so impressed me about this was Kumisi's humility. He was convinced he was right but still wanted his readers to check for themselves and not just take his word for it. He wasn't telling his readers to ignore what he said, but after they read his explanation, they needed to get the Word of God directly from Scripture without any intermediary. This approach has become my guiding philosophy for living by Scripture. I'll read what commentators and scholars have to say but I ultimately listen to what God speaks to me through His perfect Word.

The third Karaite opposition to speaking God's name was a modern one I encountered through a young Karaite rabbi, someone for whom I actually have a great deal of respect. When I shared with him the importance of speaking God's name, he went out and investigated the matter for himself. As he studied the name, he discovered that there is no scholarly consensus on its pronunciation. Theories range from Yahweh to Yihveh and everything in between. He concluded that because we are uncertain of how to pronounce God's name, we are better off not speaking it at all. His reasoning was that mispronouncing God's name would be tantamount to calling upon the name of a false god.

I understood his position. I would be the first to admit there is some degree of uncertainty about how to pronounce God's name. We don't have a recording of God speaking His name at Sinai and

---

[1] Daniel al-Kumisi, *Epistle to the Dispersion*, Oxford Bodleian, 2776/5 Ms. Heb. d. 36, folio 14a.

the scribes did their best to hide the true pronunciation from us. I am convinced that the best evidence available today tells us that the name is "Yehovah." Should better evidence be discovered, pointing to some other pronunciation, no one would be happier than me. The greatest gift God could give me is the truth. Until that happens, I have to work with what I have and pray for the Messiah to come soon in our days to reveal everything to us. I expect that he will reveal what I already believe to be true but am humble enough to allow for another possibility. I know when the Messiah sits on the throne of David as the flesh and blood king of Israel, we will all be much wiser.

The way I see it, it is better to risk *mispronouncing* God's holy name than to abandon it altogether. This was something a friend named Newman made me realize. He was a wiry young film student from Virginia spending a year at the Hebrew University. One day he joined me on a Jerusalem hillside to look for the new moon. While we waited patiently for the moon to make its first appearance on the horizon, he quietly asked me about a verse in the 44th chapter of Psalms. I had read the passage many times but never really stopped to think about what it meant. As he slowly read it to me from his English Bible, I stood there in disbelief. The Psalm was describing a time when we would be "dispersed among the nations."[1] It then went on to say that if, in our Exile, we forgot the name of God and prayed to Him using the name of a pagan deity, God would examine our hearts and still accept our prayers. I had to see this for myself in Hebrew. I pulled out an old, tattered Bible from my backpack and quickly flipped to the passage. It said the exact same thing in Hebrew that Newman read to me in English.

After the new moon sighting, I rushed home to look up the verse in the Aleppo Codex just to make sure it wasn't a misprint in my Hebrew Bible. This was such a radical statement, I decided to look at every manuscript, translation, and commentary I could get my hands on to see if there was any other legitimate way to read it. The verse literally said:

---

[1] Psalms 44:11[12].

> If we forgot the name of our God and spread forth our hands to a strange god, would not God surely investigate this, for He knows the mysteries of the heart.[1]

Some translations removed the word "if," making it a confession of a sin, rather than a hymn about God's immense mercy. This creative interpretation notwithstanding, the word "if" was clearly in all the manuscripts I examined. There was no way of getting around what the verse said, that God accepts our prayers even if through our ignorance we call Him by the wrong name.

When I read this verse, it made me think of something my grandmother, of blessed memory, used to do. She would often mix up my name with that of her eldest son, calling me "Billy." It's not that she didn't recognize me. She was just used to calling the name of my uncle and did this out of habit. When I was a boy, I resented it but years later realized this was a family trait when my sister started calling me "Nitai," the name of her firstborn son. She was a young mother who worked as a scientist, so I knew this wasn't a sign of senility. I eventually found myself doing it, calling my fifteen nephews and nieces by the wrong names. I decided the best way to save face was to use generic titles. I started referring to all my nephews as "boy" and all my nieces as "girl." I would say, "Boy, come let's go on a hike together" or "Girl, let me take you out for pizza." I thought I was being a spectacular uncle until I realized this hurt their feelings even worse than calling them by the wrong names. Now, as difficult as it is for me, I try to give them the respect they deserve by using their actual names.

Maybe this is why I am so hesitant to relegate God to nothing more than a series of generic titles. We picked up many bad habits during two thousand years of being "dispersed among the nations." We have become accustomed to calling God by His titles even though He has a perfectly good name; a name He wants us to love; a name of which Scripture says, "those who love Your name may rejoice in You."[2]

---

[1] Psalms 44:20–21[21–22].

[2] Psalms 5:11[12] [NIV], see also Isaiah 56:6; 69:36[37]; 119:132.

While I think it's important to call our Creator by His name, I am also grateful that He is not offended if we inadvertently mix up His name with that of a foreign god. It amazes me that our heavenly Father is so patient with us that He looks directly into our hearts and gives us credit for what we meant, even if it's not what we said. Wow!

This doesn't mean we should start calling on the names of Krishna, Osiris or Baal. On the contrary, God commanded us to "make no mention of the name of other gods, nor let it be heard from your mouth."[1] He expects us to do the best we can but has mercy on us when we fall short.

If God has mercy and can accept our prayers when we call Him by the *wrong* name, surely He accepts our prayers when all we do is *mispronounce* His *true* name. There *is* a special blessing in God's eternal name, but it's not a magical formula that has to be pronounced in a certain way to make our prayers effective. He will look into our hearts and know whether we did the best we could to get His name right.

I have some special insight into this, as someone with a name most people mispronounce. The proper pronunciation of my own name is N'chem-*yah*. I could count on one hand how many people pronounce my name correctly. My English-speaking friends struggle with the Hebrew letter *chet* and fumble the rest of the pronunciation while they're at it. Some call me Ne-*hee*-mee-yah while others call me Nee-hu-*my*-ah. Many Israelis also struggle with my name, pronouncing it N'*cham*-yah. Now I really don't care if people call me Ne-*hee*-mee-yah, Nee-hu-*my*-ah, or N'*cham*-yah, as long as they don't call me "baldy." The same thing is true with God's name. Ultimately, the difference between Yehovah, Yahweh, Yahuvah, Yihweh and all the other theories of how to pronounce His name are not that great. We should do the best we can to pronounce His name correctly, but even if we fumble the pronunciation, it's still better than forgetting His name altogether.

---

[1] Exodus 23:13 [NKJV].

One issue I have struggled with over the years is how to pronounce the Hebrew letter *vav* in God's name. Many scholars believe this letter was originally pronounced like the English letter W, which would make God's name "Yehowah" and not "Yehovah." As a Hebrew *speaker,* this sounds utterly ridiculous to me. Hebrew is a living language spoken by millions of people, and they all pronounce the letter *vav* like the English V.

The truth is that we don't even know for sure how the letter *vav* was pronounced thousands of years ago. No one has a recording of ancient Hebrew. What we have are multiple pronunciation traditions of different Jewish communities, and they don't agree with each other. The facts of history are that some Jewish communities in centuries past pronounced the letter *vav* as V and others pronounced it as W.[1] It's enough to make poor Tevye's head spin.

How the ancient Israelites pronounced the letter *vav* is anyone's guess. It is even possible that the different pronunciation traditions of various Jewish communities go back to ancient tribal dialects. We know that the tribe of Ephraim pronounced the Hebrew language differently from all the other tribes. The Book of Judges tells about a war in Transjordan between the tribe of Ephraim and the army of Jephthah. At the end of the war, Jephthah's men seized the fords over the Jordan River to prevent the defeated Ephraimites from returning home. Anyone attempting to cross the river was asked to pronounce the word "Shibolet." When the Ephraimites tried to say this word, it came out as "Sibolet."[2] They were unable to pronounce the "SH" sound, quite literally, to save their lives. If such a big difference existed between Ephraim and the other tribes, then it's

---

[1] Many scholars assume ancient Hebrew to be a corrupt form of Arabic and claim the Hebrew *vav* was pronounced the same as the Arabic letter *waw*. However, an 11th century Jewish manual on pronunciation proves that the Jews of the Land of Israel traditionally pronounced *vav* as V (Ilan Eldar, *Torat Hakriah Bamikra*, Jerusalem 1994, pages 65-66 [Hebrew]). This pronunciation tradition may date back to the time of Ezekiel, as can be seen, for example, from the word *gav* meaning, "back," which is sometimes written with a *vav* and sometimes with a soft *bet*, indicating that both letters were pronounced V (Ezekiel 10:2; 23:35).

[2] Judges 12:6.

possible that some ancient Israelites pronounced the letter *vav* as V and others as W.

This reminds me of something that happened many years ago to my grandmother, the one who used to call me Billy. She was a sweet, old lady who immigrated to the United States from Lithuania as a young girl. Sometime in the 1980s, she was in a minor traffic accident and the other driver got out of his car and started yelling at her. Being a true Chicagoan, my grandmother yelled back. At one point in his tirade, the other driver yelled at my grandmother, "You darn foreigner!" He didn't really say *darn.*

My grandmother didn't care about his profanity but was deeply offended that he called her a "foreigner." She had lived in Chicago longer than he had been alive. As she told me the story, she shook her head, rested her forehead in her palm, and said in her adorable Yiddish accent, "Vat made him tink I'm a fahreigner?"

If God thinks I'm a foreigner for calling Him Yehovah instead of Yehowah, I'm just fine with that. And if He thinks I talk funny because I don't pronounce His name Yahweh or Yahuah or whatever, I know He will examine my heart and find out that I am doing the best I can with the information I currently possess to love His name and rejoice in Him.

Chapter 9:

The Strong Tower

"Why are we hiking up this mountain?" the young man asked me as he sucked on a small clump of chewing tobacco. He looked out of place on the Golan Heights with his straw cowboy hat. Khaki shorts, sunglasses, and a backpack identified him as an American tourist. He had been marching along the narrow mountain trail, stumbling over rocks and ducking to avoid low-hanging branches for over an hour, and he already sweated through his brown t-shirt.

His father contacted me months earlier about taking the family around Israel, insisting they were avid hikers and didn't want the traditional air-conditioned bus tour. This was a perfect match for me. I'm not really a tour guide. I think of myself as more of a Scriptural guide.

"First and foremost," I explained to the young man in the cowboy hat, "we are walking up the mountain as a prophetic act, fulfilling the words God spoke to Abraham."

> Get up and walk to and fro in the land, through its length and its breadth, for I give it to you.[1]

God reiterated the significance of walking through the Promised Land hundreds of years later to Abraham's descendants when He said:

> Every place where the *sole of your foot* treads shall be yours; from the desert to Lebanon, and from the river—the Euphrates River—to the Western Sea shall be your border.[2]

---

[1] Genesis 13:17.

[2] Deuteronomy 11:24. The promise is repeated in Joshua 1:3.

"Walking through the land is a way of gratefully accepting this precious gift God gave our people," I concluded.

The young man was a little annoyed by my explanation and gave me a funny look.

"There's ice cream at the top!" I added enthusiastically.

This seemed to satisfy him and he picked up his pace. I had a second reason for taking the family up this particular mountainside, but I decided to wait to explain it.

About a half hour later, we reached a parking lot at the end of the mountain trail where we had left one of our rental cars earlier that day. On the other side of the parking lot was a large fortress popularly known as *Nimrod's Castle*. Despite its name, it has nothing to do with the Biblical Nimrod. The castle was built by a 13th Century Turkish general at the top of a mountain that dominates the Hula Valley in northern Israel. I told the family we could end the adventure right here or we could climb to the top of the castle. After some deliberations, the decision was made to press on. The young man in the straw hat led the way along the base of the castle walls, past the ice-cream stand, up a ramp, and over a narrow causeway that bridged a dry moat. We entered the castle through a massive gate, walked past some more fortifications, went through an inner gate and up some stairs.

Fifteen minutes later, we were taking a short breather in an inner courtyard at the base of a large square tower when I decided to explain the main reason for our journey to the castle. We are here to experience a verse in the Book of Proverbs, a verse that says:

> The name of Yehovah is a strong tower; the righteous run into it and are safe.[1]

Today we live in un-walled cities, I explained, leaving the image of a "strong tower" sounding like a bunch of meaningless words. The purpose of our hike was to experience the power and magnitude of a "strong tower." I told them how every ancient castle had a central fortification, which served as a last refuge when the outer walls were

---

[1] Proverbs 18:10.

breached. In ancient Hebrew, this was called a *migdal oz*, literally, a "strong tower." In European castles, this central fortification was called a "keep." When I said the word "keep," the eyes of the young man in the cowboy hat lit up.

"Like in *Lord of the Rings*!" he said enthusiastically.

I admitted I hadn't seen the movie.

He started to tell me about the Battle of Helm's Deep in which Saruman (the bad guy) sent his army of Uruk-hai (goblins) to capture the mountain fortress of the Hornburg (the castle), defended by Théoden of Rohan and Aragorn of Gondor (the good guys). The attackers began with a frontal assault against the outer castle walls, a diversionary tactic to distract the defenders away from the main attack. Meanwhile, a column of Uruk-hai made their way over the causeway to the outer castle gate. They used a Roman tactic, interlocking shields to form a "tortoise" shell that could repel volleys of arrows and large stones. When the column of Uruk-hai reached the gate, they used an explosive to blow a vast breach in the outer castle wall. After a brief and noble effort at holding back the enemy, the order came from King Théoden, "Aragorn! Fall back to the keep!"

Aragorn repeated the order in Elvish, "Nan Barad! Nan Barad!" which being translated means, "To the keep! Pull back to the keep!"

As the young man was telling me this, I thought to myself, "The next person who says Biblical Hebrew is complicated, needs to have a look at *The Lord of the Rings*."[1]

When the young man in the cowboy hat was done with his synopsis of the battle, a smile crept across his face. "To the keep!" he shouted, raising a fist in victory.

"To the keep!" his brother repeated excitedly, parroting the victorious arm gesture.

The two brothers ran ahead into the *migdal oz*—the keep—the castle's strong tower. I slowly lagged behind with the other family members gradually making my way up what seemed like a million steps. When we reached the top of the keep about fifteen minutes

---

[1] *The Lord of the Rings: The Two Towers*, directed by Peter Jackson, 2002.

later, the proverb really came to life. From up there, we could see the thick walls of the keep, the outer wall of the castle, the dry moat, the trail up from the base of the mountain, and the Hula valley at the foot of the mountain, where we started our hike. The view said it all. It took us two grueling hours to reach this point and this was without any resistance. An ancient army trying to capture this position would have to fight every inch of the way up the mountain, cross the moat, breach the outer walls, and only then lay siege to the strong tower. This is what the proverb meant when it said the name of Yehovah is a "strong tower." His name is not just a mountaintop fort. And it's not just a castle. It's a *migdal oz*, a strong tower, a keep—the last refuge when everything else fails. "The righteous run into it and are safe." Hallelu-Yah! Praise the name of Yehovah!

About a year earlier, I saw the "strong tower" of God's holy name in action in the life of my friend Newman. He was the one who asked me about the verse in Psalms that says God will accept our prayers, even if through our ignorance, we call Him by the wrong name. Newman got interested in his Jewish heritage when he read the Torah for the first time as a teenager. He was so moved by it that he decided to live his life by the Bible the best he could. He started wearing *tzitzit* (ritual fringes) with a blue thread, because he found this commanded in the Torah. At the same time, he was not all that interested in tradition so he didn't cover his head with a *kippah*—a skullcap, as Orthodox Jews do.

As a *kohen*, a direct descendant of Aaron the brother of Moses on his father's side, Newman took a special interest in speaking the name of God. He considered the statement at the end of the Priestly Blessing that said, "and they shall place My name upon the Children of Israel" to be a personal duty he inherited from his ancestors.[1] One concern he had, however, was the Third Commandment:

> Thou shalt not take the name of the LORD thy God in vain.[2]

---

[1] Numbers 6:27.

[2] Exodus 20:7 [KJV].

He was concerned that speaking God's holy name outside of official Temple ritual might be taking it in vain. He asked if I could use my expertise in ancient Hebrew to help him understand this commandment.

I explained to Newman that in ancient Hebrew the word "vain" is often a synonym for "false."[1] Taking God's name "in vain" means to speak His name *falsely*. The ancient Israelites used to open their vows with the words, "as Yehovah lives." Following those words with a lie would be taking God's name falsely—*in vain*.

"This is the ancient Jewish understanding of the verse found in some of our earliest sources," I concluded.[2]

A few months later, Newman had the opportunity to speak Yehovah's name truthfully, as truthfully and sincerely as anyone ever spoke it. It happened one night when he joined some friends and me to watch the classic Humphrey Bogart movie *Casablanca*.[3] After the movie, he decided to walk back to his dorm room and got lost. Before Newman knew it, he was walking through a forest on the edge of Jerusalem. As he walked down the dark trail, he turned a corner and found himself standing in a clearing, face-to-face with three Arabs. They saw his *tzitzit*, his ritual fringes, and immediately recognized him as a Jew. Two of them grabbed Newman by his arms, while the third started to swing a knife at him. The first cut sliced through his neck, nicking his jugular vein. The second landed on the left side of his face cutting a deep gash from ear to mouth. At that moment, Newman believed he was going to die, that he was about to take his last breath. As his attacker swung the knife a third time to finish him off, Newman cried out to God, shouting at the top of his lungs, "Yehovah!!!" The next thing Newman knew, he was running through the forest. He had no idea how he got free. He just ran. When he reached the edge of the forest, he realized blood was gushing from his neck. He quickly took off his shirt and pressed it

---

1 For example, compare the Hebrew of the Ninth Commandment in Exodus 20:16 [verse 13 in some versions] with Deuteronomy 5:20 [verse 17 in some versions].

2 *Babylonian Talmud*, Shavuot 20b; for more sources, see *A Prayer to Our Father*, pages 104–105.

3 *Casablanca*, directed by Michael Curtiz, 1942.

tightly against the wound. Later at the hospital, they told him if the knife had penetrated even a fraction of an inch deeper, he would have died right there in the forest. Newman ran into the *migdal oz*, the strong tower of God's holy name, and was safe!

In the late 1800s, the Lakota Sioux used to perform a ritual called the "ghost dance." Some of them believed the shirts worn during this dance became imbued with powerful spiritual forces that could repel bullets. While God's name can bring blessings upon us, it does not work like a Lakota "ghost shirt." Calling on His name doesn't guarantee you will be safe or blessed. Rabbi Hanina ben Teradion lost his life precisely because he spoke God's holy name. It would be easy to condemn Rabbi Hanina, to say he wasn't protected because of some sin in his life. Over the years, I've encountered many people who believe bad things only happen to bad people, whereas if you are righteous God will always protect you from harm. I remember when I was in elementary school a young Jewish girl my age died of cancer. The town gossips went around saying it was because her family wasn't religious enough. Or because she wore pants and short-sleeve shirts. Or because her father's *tefillin* (phylacteries) were defective.[1]

Today, I know this gossip and condemnation was sinful in its own right. This was exactly the sin of Job's three companions. When Job suffered the loss of property, loved ones, and finally his own health, his three companions denounced him as a sinner, demanding that he repent. They believed that all human suffering was the direct and automatic result of sin, that anyone who suffered must be a sinner whom God was punishing. Towards the end of the Book of Job, God appeared to the companions and condemned them:

> My wrath is kindled against you… for you have not spoken of Me what is right.[2]

---

[1] *Tefillin* consist of two black cubes that Jewish men traditionally strap to their arm and forehead during morning prayers. The black cubes contain tiny scrolls inscribed with biblical passages. The *tefillin* are deemed "defective" if the ink on the scrolls fades or they contain a spelling mistake.

[2] Job 42:7 [NRSV].

Job's three companions failed to understand what King Solomon observed in the Book of Ecclesiastes:

> There is a just man who perishes in his righteousness, and there is a wicked man who prolongs life in his wickedness.[1]

In plain English: bad things sometimes happen to good people. And good things sometimes happen to bad people. Living by the Word of God is not some sort of Hebraic *karma*. The one thing we can be confident in is that justice will ultimately prevail, if not in this world then in the next. This was Solomon's conclusion at the end of Ecclesiastes:

> The end of the matter; all has been heard. Fear God, and keep His commandments; for that is the whole of man. For God will bring every deed into judgment, including every secret thing, whether good or evil.[2]

Solomon was saying we need to do what is right and trust that God will do justice on the Day of Judgment. Rabbi Hanina understood this and that's why he was willing to risk martyrdom at the hands of the Romans by speaking God's holy name. He knew that if he died he would be inscribed in the "Book of Remembrance" in the world to come. He was actually famous for a saying that testified to this, a saying quoted in *Ethics of the Fathers*:

> When two sit together and exchange words of Torah, the *Shechinah* is among them, as it is written, "Then those who fear Yehovah spoke one to another and Yehovah heard and listened and a Book of Remembrance was inscribed in His presence for those who fear Yehovah *and meditate upon His name*."[3]

The concept of the *Shechinah* appears in the Hebrew Bible when it says that God "causes His name to dwell" in the Tabernacle and later

---

[1] Ecclesiastes 7:15 [NKJV].
[2] Ecclesiastes 12:13–14 [NRSV].
[3] *Ethics of the Fathers* 3:2 quoting Malachi 3:16.

in the Temple.[1] The Hebrew word for "dwell" is *shaken* (pronounced *shah-ken*), and this is the source of the word *Shechinah*, which means, "indwelling." The broadest definition of the *Shechinah* or *indwelling* of God's name is something about God we can experience in a tangible way. God was felt in the Tabernacle and the Temple in a way he was not normally experienced anywhere else. Rabbi Hanina was saying that the *Shechinah*, the indwelling of God's name is experienced not only in the Temple but also wherever two people gather to speak about the Word of God *and meditate upon His name.* God Himself confirms this when he says in Exodus:

> …in every place where I cause My name to be mentioned, I will come to you and bless you.[2]

Rabbi Hanina fearlessly defied the Roman decree against teaching Torah and speaking God's name in public, because he knew this would bring a blessing. Even if he lost his life, he knew his name would be recorded in the Book of Remembrance before God.

The Almighty *will* bless every person who calls upon His name in sincerity and humility. And He *will* bless every place where His name is mentioned in truth and righteousness. However, His name is not a magical mantra that guarantees we'll always get what we want in this world. Some of these blessings may be received only in the next world.

When the blessings do manifest in this world, they are great testimony to God. I recently saw such a testimony at a place where God's holy name was mentioned. It was the day I spent in New York after the Jewish Book Council, waiting for my plane back to Tel Aviv. That morning I took the ferry to Ellis Island. When I arrived back in Battery Park at the southern end of Manhattan, I walked over to Ground Zero. Ground Zero was where those terrible events happened years earlier. That was the day I was sitting in Jerusalem examining a Hebrew manuscript of the Bible, the day I found the pronunciation of God's holy name in the Aleppo Codex.

---

[1] Deuteronomy 12:11. Also Deuteronomy 12:5; 14:23; 16:2; 16:6, 11; 26:2; Jeremiah 17:2; Nehemiah 1:9.

[2] Exodus 20:24 [NJPS].

My first reaction to Ground Zero was disappointment. In some macabre way, I expected to see the massive smoldering hole in the ground, the one I'd seen a thousand times on television. It was before the 9/11 memorial was built and all I found was a chain-link fence covered in a series of blue tarps. I could hear the earth humming with activity from behind the fence as the new Freedom Tower slowly rose from the ruins, but I could not see anything other than a few cranes peeking out from behind the barrier. I spent a few minutes in silent prayer while staring at the blue tarp and then turned around and made my way across Church Street.

My next stop was a rather unusual one for a Jew, a historic church located only 300 yards away from where the Twin Towers once stood. Most tourists come to St. Paul's Chapel, built in 1766, to see the wooden pew where George Washington used to worship when he was president. I was not interested in that. I heard a story about this chapel I needed to check out for myself. I had already confirmed the chapel survived, undamaged from the deluge of pulverized steel and concrete that swept through the area on 9/11. Not a single window was broken that day. I approached the rear facade of the church and looked skyward to the 218-foot steeple. Here was a veritable *migdal oz*, a strong tower that survived the apocalypse of 9/11 when the two towers across the street came crashing down.

I walked in through the rear entrance and immediately spotted what I came to see. Instead of the giant cross that adorns the front of most churches, St. Paul's chapel had a beautiful sculpture of Mount Sinai, the work of Pierre L'Enfant, the architect who also designed Washington, D.C. At the bottom of the sculpture were the Ten Commandments on two black tablets written in English with golden letters. Above the tablets, up at the top of Mount Sinai, was the name of God, Yod-Hay-Vav-Hay, in black Hebrew letters, surrounded by golden rays of light. God's holy name appeared a second time in black Hebrew letters, high above the sculpture of Mount Sinai, adorning the keystone of an arch. I couldn't believe it. The name "Yehovah" was inscribed twice in large black Hebrew letters at the front of an Episcopal chapel. And this was the second time I encountered God's name at the top of "Mount Sinai." This Sinai was tied intimately to my own discovery of the pronunciation of God's holy name. At the very moment I was poring over the Aleppo Codex looking for the name of Yehovah 6,000 miles away, this strong tower, a place where he caused His name to be mentioned, was withstanding the cataclysm of that tragic day. Some of the survivors of 9/11 quite literally ran into it and were safe. One of them was NYPD detective David Brink who was engulfed in the debris cloud when the south tower collapsed. He eventually found refuge in St. Paul's Chapel, where he used "holy water" to wash the toxic dust out of his eyes.

"All we wanted to do was find some clean air to breathe," Brink later remembered.[1]

I stood there staring at Yehovah's name, thinking about the senseless murder of all those innocent people. I felt a deep tension about God miraculously sparing this building while thousands died across the street. Reverend Lyndon Harris, a clergyman at St. Paul's Chapel, wrote something profound in *National Geographic* that helped me come to terms with this:

> Opening the door to enter St. Paul's [on September 12, 2001] was an extraordinary experience; except for a layer of ash and soot, the building survived unscathed. Many proclaimed that "St. Paul's had been spared." It seemed clear to me that if this was true, it was not because we were holier than anyone who died across the street; it was because we now had a big job to do.[2]

The "big job" Reverend Harris referred to was serving as a rest area for rescue-and-recovery workers searching for survivors and clearing away debris. Even Washington's historic pew was turned into a makeshift doctor's office to treat rescue workers whose feet were burned by smoldering rubble. This little chapel with God's name became a tower of hope in the middle of unimaginable tragedy, a

---

1 Brink's testimony is recorded at http://broadcastr.com/.

2 http://ngm.nationalgeographic.com/ngm/0209/st_pauls/online_extra.html

testimony to His great name, and an architectural fulfillment of the verse:

> That men may know that You, whose name alone is Yehovah, are the most high over all the earth.[1]

I'm convinced God wants His name to be known. The time for secrets is over. It's time to shout, "To the keep!" with our fists raised in victory and run into the strong tower of God's holy name. It's time to answer the call of the Psalmist, to "give thanks to Yehovah, call upon His name, make known His deeds among the nations."[2]

---

[1] Psalms 83:18[19] [adapted from KJV].
[2] Psalms 105:1; see also 1 Chronicles 16:8.

Chapter 10:

The Double Portion

I was deep in the heart of the West Bank looking for a valley mentioned only once in the Bible, the *Valley of Blessing*. My search for this valley came a few months after visiting Ground Zero. Being in the place where so many were cut off in their prime got me thinking about my own mortality and how blessed I was just to be alive. I kept coming back to the opening words of the Priestly Blessing—"May Yehovah bless you."[1] I wondered whether this was really about God blessing us with *physical* things. In the wake of so much carnage, I felt guilty asking God to bless me with health, wealth, a loving family, and happiness. I would find myself deep in prayer and get this image of myself as Cuba Gooding Jr. in the movie *Jerry Maguire*. I would be on the phone with my sports agent yelling at the top of my lungs, "Show me the money! Show me the money!"[2] This is what I imagined myself sounding like to God, pestering Him with my prayers and requests. Were my petty problems and issues important enough to bother the Creator of the Universe when so many died senseless deaths?

I decided the only way to resolve the tension I was feeling was to figure out what it means in the Hebrew Bible *for God to bless us*. I touched upon the exact opposite question in my book on the "Lord's Prayer," exploring what it means *for us to bless God*. I found the key to understanding this in the root of the Hebrew word for "blessing." Some people start to tune out or fall asleep when they hear about Hebrew roots and their meanings, but I love this stuff. The Hebrew language is fascinating to me. God used it to reveal His will to

---

[1] Numbers 6:24.

[2] *Jerry Maguire*, directed by Cameron Crowe, 1996.

mankind, and I believe understanding its nuances gives us a glimpse into the mind of God and His plan for our lives.

The concept of how we bless God is a great example of the power of meaning that Hebrew roots unlock. The Hebrew word for "blessing" comes from the root *bet-resh-kaf*, which literally means "knee." Ancient Hebrew connected most abstract concepts to concrete tangible things from everyday life. In plain English, this means *ideas* are linked to things we can *see* or *touch*. If you think about it, "blessing" is an abstract concept, an idea. You can see the results of a "blessing," but you can't see or touch the "blessing" itself. In contrast, a "knee" is about as concrete and tangible as you can get. In the most basic sense, to bless God means to bow down on your "knees" in His presence. In ancient times, people would bless a king by kneeling down on their knees and praising Him. This doesn't mean you have to kneel down every time you bless God but understanding the origin of the word breathes life and color into it.[1]

God blessing His creations must have a different connection to the word "knee." Obviously, God doesn't kneel down before us and neither would an ancient king kneel down before his subjects. So what does it mean for God to *bless* His people? I wasn't certain I would find an answer. Studying an ancient language can be tricky and you don't always get definitive results.

I started looking for clues at the beginning of the Bible, in the Book of Genesis, which records a series of blessings of fathers to their sons. I knew this was important because Scripture symbolically describes God's relationship with us as that of a father with his son. One fatherly blessing that caught my attention was when Joseph brought his two sons to Jacob to be blessed. Jacob placed one hand on each of his grandchildren and blessed them with the words:

> By you Israel will bless, saying, "May God make you as Ephraim and as Manasseh."[2]

---

[1] See *A Prayer to Our Father*, pages 124–125.

[2] Genesis 48:20 [NKJV].

The significance of this blessing was that Jacob gave his grandsons full portions of inheritance as if they were his actual sons. This meant that Joseph was receiving a *double portion* of inheritance through his two boys. Blessing someone with the words, "May God make you as Ephraim and as Manasseh," is praying that they receive a double portion of inheritance from God. My father used to bless me with these exact words every Friday night, placing his hand on my head just as Jacob did to his two grandsons.

The key detail in the story was when Joseph first presented his two sons to Jacob. Apparently, they were still young, so Joseph sat each boy down on one of his *knees*.[1] It occurred to me that the concrete, tangible meaning of "knee" was connected to a father blessing his young child by sitting him down on his knee. This meant that when God blesses us He is sitting us down like little children on His knees, placing His hand on our heads, and wishing our success and well-being. What a powerful picture of fatherhood!

I wanted to know more. I started to look closely at the blessings each of the forefathers gave to their sons. Competing for this blessing was a central point of contention between the fraternal twins Jacob and Esau. As the firstborn, Esau was entitled to a double portion of inheritance from his father. Esau didn't appreciate his birthright and sold it for a bowl of red lentil stew. Despite this foolhardy move, when the day came for their father's blessing, Esau had no intention of giving up his double portion. This forced Jacob to take through deception what should have been his by right. When Esau discovered this deception, he asked his father, Isaac for whatever blessing he had left.

As I carefully read the blessing that Isaac finally gave Esau, I noticed that it didn't sound all that different from his blessing to Jacob. Both seemed to be purely physical blessings of economic prosperity and political sovereignty. There was one minor difference, a difference I might have easily missed had I not read all the blessings of the forefathers. It was at the end of the blessing to Jacob, where Isaac said:

---

[1] Genesis 48:12.

> …those who curse you will be cursed and those who bless you will be blessed.[1]

This seemingly innocuous statement is extremely significant. This was the exact same blessing God gave to Abraham earlier in Genesis, a blessing of God's friendship and protection. It was God's way of saying, "Any friend of Abraham's is a friend of mine and any enemy of his is an enemy of mine." In that same blessing of friendship and protection, God promised Abraham that He would make him into a great nation, a nation that would eventually bring blessing upon "all the families of the earth."[2]

It was an Arab Christian, a few months earlier, who made me realize how amazing this blessing to Abraham was. Some mutual friends brought me over to meet him at his apartment in southern Jerusalem. The Arab man greeted me with some tea and cake, then immediately launched into his testimony. He told me that he was born into a family of Arab Christians and raised to hate Israel and the Jews. One day he was praying on the Mount of Olives when he heard a voice ask him, "Why do you say you love Me when you hate My people?" He then heard God's promise to Abraham, "I will bless those who bless you and curse those who curse you."[3] At that moment, he realized he was under a curse for hating Abraham's descendants.

From that day forward, this Arab Christian man began to preach to love Israel and the Jews to anyone who would listen. He understood that the Jews are the rightful heirs to Abraham's promise and covenant, handed down through Isaac and Jacob.

This was the importance of the blessing, "those who curse you will be cursed and those who bless you will be blessed." Isaac was blessing Jacob as the rightful heir to God's promise and covenant with Abraham. Esau might have received the physical blessing of being prosperous, but he did not inherit the blessing of Abraham's covenant as Jacob did. Esau received a single portion of inheritance,

---

[1] Genesis 27:29.
[2] Genesis 12:3.
[3] Genesis 12:3.

the physical blessing alone. Jacob received his rightful double portion of inheritance consisting of both the physical blessing and the spiritual blessing.[1]

After Jacob received the double portion, he fled from the Land of Canaan to avoid the vengeance of his brother Esau. On the way, he stopped off at Bethel where he made a vow and prayed to God, asking his Creator to:

> …protect me on this way that I go, and give me *food* to eat and *clothing* to wear, so that I return in peace to the house of my father…[2]

If Cuba Gooding Jr. were to play Jacob in the movie version, he'd be yelling at the top of his lungs, "Show me the bread and show me the thread!" Only a few verses earlier God promised Jacob He would be with him, care for him, and return him home safely.[3] I thought it was profound that even after this promise, Jacob didn't take God's blessing for granted and still prayed for it.

As I continued my search through the Bible, I found numerous examples like this of people asking God for physical blessings. There was Hannah who asked for a son, David who asked for victory, and Jabez who prayed for an enlarged border. Towards the end of my study, I read in the Book of Chronicles about a place called the "Valley of Blessing." I immediately knew I needed to go there and see it for myself.

Finding the Valley of Blessing was relatively easy. The location is immortalized in the name of a nearby mound called the Ruin of Blessing. As I stood atop a hill, overlooking the Valley of Blessing, I re-read the Biblical account. The story in the Book of Chronicles starts with an invasion force landing on the western shore of the Dead Sea. This foreign coalition of Ammonites, Moabites, and Edomites slipped past border fortifications by marching up a dry riverbed, threatening the very heart of the Kingdom of Judah.

---

[1] Isaac reiterated that Jacob would be the heir to God's promise to Abraham in Genesis 28:4 and God Himself confirmed this in Genesis 28:13–15.

[2] Genesis 28:20–21.

[3] Genesis 28:15.

The army of Judah led by King Jehoshaphat went out to fight the invaders but never arrived at the battlefield. Instead, they saw these three foreign armies turn on one another, sending their forces scattering into the countryside. All that remained for Jehoshaphat to do was plunder the abandoned enemy army camps. The spoils were so great his men took three days to gather them all up. On the fourth day, the army of Judah regrouped in a valley eleven miles southwest of Jerusalem. In that valley they blessed God and "therefore they called the name of that place Emek Berachah (Valley of Blessing) until today."[1]

The express reason given for the name "Valley of Blessing" was that Jehoshaphat blessed God. However, like many names in the Bible there was a second reason for the name, one implied in the passage but no less valid than the reason expressly stated. The *implicit* reason for the name Valley of Blessing was that God blessed the Israelites by defeating their enemies and allowing them to gather up the spoils of war. The Valley of Blessing signified not only man blessing God but also God blessing man. The main reason Jehoshaphat blessed God in the valley was the victory and spoils with which God blessed him.

Standing on that hillside overlooking the Valley of Blessing, I realized there was a third reason for the name implied in the very landscape. The picturesque Valley of Blessing is covered in endless rows of grapevines and blessed with a fertility that stands out at the edge of the Judean Desert. I could see Jehoshaphat millennia ago, bent down among the grapevines with his knees pressed into the fertile soil and his hands raised towards heaven, blessing God for victory and the spoils of war. The Valley of Blessing celebrates not only man blessing God but also God blessing man with a purely *physical* blessing of fertility, wealth, and victory.

In Israel, whenever you encounter the physical, the spiritual is never too far away. The Valley of Blessing was no exception. My vantage point overlooking the valley was on the outskirts of a tranquil, little Jewish town called Migdal Oz, "Strong Tower." It was

---

[1] 2 Chronicles 20:26.

named after the verse in Proverbs that had brought me to Ground Zero, the verse that said, "The name of Yehovah is a strong tower; the righteous run into it and are safe."[1] I started jumping with excitement when I realized I was witnessing a geographical manifestation of Jacob's double portion of inheritance: the Strong Tower and the Valley of Blessing. The spiritual blessing of God's holy name towering over the physical blessing of fertility, victory, and wealth. What a powerful picture of God's providence!

Being at the Valley of Blessing, side-by-side with Migdal Oz, got me thinking about the spiritual blessing God guarantees even when He withholds the physical blessing. I knew there was another valley in Israel related to the ultimate spiritual blessing, *eternal life*. I learned about this other valley years earlier when my grandmother was terminally ill. Her impending death was the first time in my life I ever had to deal with the passing of a close loved one. I found myself asking what would happen to her after she died. By this time, I had begun down the Karaite path, so the traditional explanations didn't satisfy me. I went back to Scripture to find answers. The key passage was in the 133rd chapter of Psalms, which spoke about the mountains of Zion and then said, "for there Yehovah commanded the blessing of eternal life."[2]

What did it mean that God commanded the blessing of eternal life in the mountains of Zion? I knew that Jerusalem, the ancient capital of Israel, was located in the mountains of Zion. This is why Jews like me who believe God gave us the Land of Israel are called "Zionists." But what did Zion—Jerusalem—have to do with eternal life? As I continued my search, I found a clue in the Book of Daniel, which said:

> Many of those who sleep in the dust of the earth shall arise, some to eternal life and some to shame, to eternal contempt.[3]

---

[1] Proverbs 18:10.

[2] Psalms 133:3.

[3] Daniel 12:2.

Daniel was speaking about the future resurrection of the dead and the final judgment in which the righteous will be rewarded with *eternal life*. Jews often refer to this future existence as *Olam Haba*—the World to Come. But what did Olam Haba have to do with Jerusalem? I finally found the answer in the Book of Joel, which describes this final judgment:

> For behold in those days and at that time… the nations will awaken and go up to the Valley of Jehoshaphat, for there I will sit to judge all the nations roundabout.[1]

I immediately knew that "Valley of Jehoshaphat" was a play on words. Jehoshaphat means "Yehovah Judges." Joel was saying that the final judgment will take place in the Valley of Yehovah's Judgment, referred to later in the same prophecy as the Valley of Decision.[2]

Some quick research identified the location of the Valley of Decision. It ran through the heart of modern Jerusalem separating the Temple Mount from the Mount of Olives, covering the northern end of the Kidron Valley. For centuries, Jews have come from all over the world to be buried on the Mount of Olives, on the eastern slope of the Valley of Decision so that they could be near the epicenter of the resurrection when it begins. This is what the Psalms meant when it said, "for there Yehovah commanded the blessing of eternal life." There, in the Valley of Decision, among the mountains of Zion, the dead will be resurrected and God will carry out His judgment, *blessing the righteous with eternal life*. Today this slope is covered with tens of thousands of gleaming-white marble tombstones testifying to millennia of Jewish faith in the final resurrection and the reward of eternal life that will one day be granted in the valley below. This was a great comfort to me, knowing I would see my grandmother once again in the Valley of Decision when we both stand before our Creator on the Day of Judgment.

---

[1] Joel 3:1–2[4:1–2]; 3:12[4:12]. The verse says that the nations will go "up" to the valley because in Hebrew going to Jerusalem is described as an "ascent" (for example, 1 Kings 12:28). This is why immigration to Israel is called *Aliyah*, literally "ascent."
[2] Joel 3:14[4:14].

A few weeks after my visit to the Valley of Blessing, I decided to head over to the Valley of Jehoshaphat. I'd been there countless times before, but this time I took my Bible so I could re-read the prophecy in Joel on the very spot it would be fulfilled. I got goose bumps reading one particular verse towards the end of the prophecy:

> Yehovah roars from Zion, and utters His voice from Jerusalem, and the heavens and the earth shake. But Yehovah is a refuge for His people, a stronghold (*maoz*) for the people of Israel.[1]

I looked down across the valley and could see it happening in my mind's eye: God sitting in judgment before all mankind; the earth quaking at His voice like it did at Sinai; and on that day, God being a mighty stronghold for His people. I started panting in excitement when the Hebrew word for "stronghold" jumped off the page. The word was *maoz* from the same root as *migdal oz*, strong tower! On that day, God will be a *maoz*, a stronghold in the valley for His people!

Having been to both valleys, I'm now comfortable praying to God to "please, show me the blessings!" I don't feel guilty anymore asking my Creator for the same blessings that moved Jehoshaphat to bless God in the Valley of Blessing—physical blessings such as health, wealth, family, and happiness. But whether I get these physical blessings or not, I have faith in the blessing God promised He would give in that other valley, the Valley of Decision, the blessing of eternal life. I pray that God grant me a portion in the Valley of Blessing and look forward to that great and awesome day in the Valley of Decision.

---

[1] Joel 3:16[4:16] [adapted from NRSV].

Chapter 11:

God-incidences Hidden and Revealed

The tired slaves reeled in horror at the volley of arrows so numerous they blocked out the sun. The projectiles would land any second, strewing death and destruction across the broad sand-peninsula. Trapped between the sea and the Egyptian army, there was nowhere to run. Suddenly, a thick grey cloud came billowing down from the heavens, covering the tired pilgrims with its protection. The pillar of cloud silently absorbed the arrows, protecting the Israelites from their deadly sting.

When I was a child in the synagogue, hearing the Aaronic priests bless the congregation with the words, "may the LORD… protect you," I always thought of God performing a supernatural miracle like the pillar of cloud.[1] Although I've never seen a pillar of cloud myself, I have experienced God's protection all the same. The God-protection incident that stands out for me more than any other event took place during the "Second Intifada." That was the ruthless terror war, which the Palestinians waged against Israeli civilians for five years beginning in September 2000. Those were tough times. I remember that the nightly news would open with: "The following were the terrorist attacks for the day." They would then list the attacks in which people were killed or wounded. The foiled and failed terror strikes were innumerable and usually went unreported.

My miracle came one September night when I was out walking my dog, Georgia. She was running circles around me, marking every tree and stone in her path with her canine scent. When we reached the end of the old train tracks in south Jerusalem, we cut across a side alley and then turned down Emek Refaim, a historic street where David fought the Philistines. Georgia hurriedly went about her

---

[1] Numbers 6:24.

business, oblivious to the battles that once raged there. As she scurried from tree to tree, I peacefully strolled past the bustling cafés and bistros. When we reached the Hillel Café, we took a hard left and headed about 500 feet back to my apartment. A few minutes later, I was sitting in front of my computer reading e-mails and winding down before going to sleep. A shockwave shattered the quiet of the Jerusalem night when the suicide bomber detonated his explosive vest. The tree across the street was still dripping with Georgia's canine markings when it was sprayed by flying glass, pulverized bone, and blood. The blast ripped the Hillel Café wide open, killing seven and wounding over fifty.

If I had walked by a few minutes later, I might have been one of the victims that night. Instead, God carried out the Priestly Blessing in my life as I experienced the words, "May Yehovah… protect you." This protection didn't appear as a pillar of cloud coming down from heaven. There was no obvious suspension of the laws of nature. God's protection was more subtle. It took the form of a series of small events that added up to my being out of harm's way: *an upsetting e-mail that sent me out a few minutes early on my walk. Georgia running down the train tracks at record speed to wolf down the mummified remains of a discarded falafel sandwich. My fleeing the yells of an old woman upset that I didn't have my pooch on a leash.* The net effect was that I was safely back at home when the bomb detonated. Any of the individual events that led to this outcome could be dismissed as mere coincidence. However, when coincidences like this add up, I no longer consider them coincidences. I call them "God-incidences." I see this as God intervening in my life from behind the scenes as He so often did in the history of Israel.

The Torah talks about God-incidences—the protection God provides by acting from behind the scenes—in the story of Joseph, who was sold into slavery by his brothers. When Joseph became viceroy of Egypt years later, his brothers stood before him, terrified that he would exact revenge for what they did to him. In the Torah, forcibly selling someone into slavery is punishable by death, so

Joseph was within his rights to order them to be executed.[1] Instead, what the brothers intended for evil, God used for His own good purpose, as Joseph explained:

> …do not be sad and do not be upset that you sold me here, for *God sent me* before you to save life… to place a remnant in the earth and to save your lives by a great rescue. And now, *you did not send me here, but God…*[2]

When Joseph said to his brothers "you did not send me here, but God" this wasn't, strictly speaking, true. The brothers did sell Joseph into slavery. What Joseph meant was that his brothers did not realize that God was influencing the long-term outcome of events to place Joseph in a position where he could rescue his entire family. God didn't do this through an overt supernatural miracle like the pillar of cloud. Rather, through a series of perfectly timed, everyday events, He influenced everything to turn out just right.

It started with Joseph having a dream that his brothers would bow down before him. This aroused their hatred and resulted in their desire to kill him. Just as the brothers were about to murder Joseph, they saw a caravan of slave traders and decided to sell him. The slave-traders brought Joseph down to Egypt and sold him to one of Pharaoh's officials. As a slave in Egypt, Joseph became chief steward of his master's house. The lady of the house tried to seduce him and when he spurned her advances, she accused him of attacking her. Joseph was thrown into a dungeon where he met two servants of the king and interpreted their dreams.

Two years later, when the king had his own disturbing dreams, one of the servants who had been in the dungeon told the king about Joseph. He then interpreted Pharaoh's dreams, revealing to the king that Egypt would experience seven years of plenty followed by seven years of famine. Joseph also gave advice to Pharaoh on how to survive the coming famine. Seeing how wise Joseph was, the king appointed him as viceroy. Years later, when Joseph was overseeing

---

[1] Exodus 21:16; Deuteronomy 24:7.

[2] Genesis 45:5, 7–8.

the sale of grain during the famine, his brothers appeared and bowed down before him in accordance with Egyptian custom. Joseph recognized his brothers, but they did not recognize him. After testing them to see if they had repented for selling him into slavery, Joseph revealed himself to his brothers and invited them to come to Egypt where they would be saved from the famine. Any one of these events, by itself, could have been explained away as a coincidence, but they cumulatively add up to God-incidences—God performing the protection promised in the Priestly Blessing by influencing the course of events from behind the scenes.

The Jewish sages called this type of divine intervention *hester panim*, meaning "hidden face." They derived this concept from the Book of Deuteronomy in a passage that talks about how God will treat the Israelites when they sin against Him:

> My anger shall burn against them on that day and I will leave them and hide (*histarti*) My face from them and they shall become prey and many distressing evils shall find them... And I will surely hide (*haster 'astir*) My face on that day because of all the evil he has done...[1]

When God refers to *hiding* His *face*, He means He will stand back and allow bad things to happen to us as a punishment for our sins. It also means that when God does intervene, it is in a *hidden* manner. Instead of overt, obvious miracles that suspend the laws of nature (like the pillar of cloud), when God hides His face, He acts in a hidden manner by subtly influencing countless events with precise timing. This is what Isaiah meant when he said:

> You are surely God, who hides Himself (*mistater*), the God of Israel, who saves.[2]

In the story of Joseph, God's role is primarily "hidden," as He acts through *hester panim*—the "hidden face"—saving Egypt, Canaan, and Israel.

---

[1] Deuteronomy 31:17–18. See also Deuteronomy 32:20; Isaiah 8:17; 45:15, 54:8; 64:7[6]; Jeremiah 33:5; Ezekiel 39:23, etc.

[2] Isaiah 45:15.

God's protection through the "hidden face" is the opposite of another part of the Priestly Blessing, the part usually translated, "The LORD lift up His countenance upon thee."[1] In Hebrew, it literally says, "May Yehovah lift His face towards you."

I heard this blessing my entire life and didn't know what it meant until one day during a lecture at the Hebrew University one of my professors said, "God is missing from the Scroll of Esther." He was talking about the Book of Esther in the Tanakh, which in Hebrew is referred to as a *megillah*, a "scroll."

When the professor said this about the Scroll of Esther, I looked up from the notebook in which I was scribbling and put down my pen. *"Did he just say God is 'missing' from the Scroll of Esther?"* I thought. I caught myself subconsciously raising an eyebrow in surprise and confusion, the way Mr. Spock used to do in *Star Trek*.

After a brief pause, the professor explained that there is not a single direct reference to God anywhere in the Scroll of Esther. This bothered the ancient Greek translators so much that they added verses in their translation, inserting God into the text. However, in the original Hebrew, God simply was not mentioned.

At first, I did not believe him. I went home that night and read Esther from beginning to end. Not only was there no mention of God's name "Yehovah" anywhere in the scroll but the words "God," "Lord," and all of His other titles were totally absent.

"Curious," I muttered to myself in my Spock voice.

I read the scroll a second time. Then a third time. God really was missing from an entire book of the Hebrew Bible!

"Most illogical!" I finally blurted out.

I needed answers and began an in-depth study of the Scroll of Esther. The scroll tells the story of Haman's plot to wipe out the Jews in the Persian Empire. This famous story is dramatized in the Hollywood movie *One Night with the King*. The movie portrays Haman as a maniacal demagogue, motivated by an ancestral hatred, who incites large crowds against the Jews with his inflammatory speeches. In short, Haman is a prototype for Hitler. This two-dimensional

---

[1] Numbers 6:26 [KJV].

caricature of the villain has little to do with the historical Haman recorded in the Bible. The Biblical Haman was a vicious racist, to be sure, but he was not motivated by an ancestral hatred as in the movie.[1] The Haman of history hated the Jews because of a perceived slight from one Jew, Mordechai, who refused to prostrate before him. When he learned that Mordechai's refusal was due to his Jewish faith, which forbade him to worship a human being, Haman vowed to wipe out all of the Jews.

In many ways, the story of Esther in the Bible resembles that of Joseph. In the Scroll of Esther, God brings about Israel's salvation from Haman's evil plot through a long series of events spread out over many years, continually acting from behind the scenes. The series of events began with a drunken banquet held by King Ahasuerus in which he banished his queen. When the king sobered up, he began the search for a new queen and eventually chose Esther, Mordecai's niece. While Mordecai was keeping an eye on his niece, he spent a great deal of time in front of the royal palace where he happened to overhear a plot to kill the king. He reported the plot to the proper authorities who recorded what happened in the royal annals.

While spending time in front of the palace, Mordecai encountered Haman for the first time and refused to prostrate before him. When Mordecai learned of Haman's genocidal plot, he asked Esther to approach the king about rescinding the order. Esther attempted to arouse the king's jealousy by holding a banquet with Haman and him as the only two guests. At the banquet, Esther announced a second banquet to be held the following day, again with the king and Haman as the only two guests. This further aroused the king's jealousy. Haman was elated to be invited to these banquets but distraught that Mordecai continued to refuse to prostrate to him.

---

[1] *One Night with the King*, directed by Michael O. Sajbel, 2006. A rabbinical tradition labels Haman as an Amalekite based on his identification as an "Agagite," which they interpret to mean he is a descendant of Agag King of Amalek (*Babylonian Talmud*, Megilah 13a). However, the term Agagite may identify Haman as hailing from the basin of the Aegean Sea. The ancient Greek translation accordingly translates Agagite as "Macedonian," a nation located in antiquity on the northern shore of the Aegean (LXX Esther 9:24; 16:10, 14).

Seeking counsel from his loved ones, Haman decided to prepare a gallows to hang Mordecai.

That night, the king had trouble sleeping and asked that the royal annals be read to him and he learned of the assassination plot uncovered by Mordecai. The next morning, just as the king was trying to decide how to reward Mordecai, Haman arrived at the royal court to ask permission to hang him. Instead of hanging Mordechai, Haman ended up leading him through Susa on a royal horse proclaiming, "Thus shall be done to the man whom the king wishes to honor."[1] This unexpected development was devastating to Haman, who returned home where those close to him told him he was probably doomed.

At that very moment, before Haman realized what was happening, the king's men rushed him off to Esther's second banquet, where she revealed herself a Jew. She told the king how Haman wanted to wipe out her entire race. Naturally, the king was upset and walked out to his garden. When he returned, he found Haman prostrate on Esther's bed begging for mercy. The king was already suspicious of Haman for being the only other guest at his wife's banquets, and he now assumed that Haman was either making advances on her or trying to kill her. At that moment, one of the king's men pointed out of the window to the gallows, which Haman had prepared with the intention of executing Mordecai. The king was livid that Haman was preparing to execute the very man he honored earlier that day and ordered Haman to be hanged immediately. He then took the royal signet ring off Haman's finger and gave it to Mordecai, who sent out letters to the Jews giving them permission to defend themselves on the day of the impending attack. The attack came and the Jews were victorious.

Purim was always one of my favorite Jewish holidays. I loved dressing up in different costumes, a Jewish tradition that symbolizes the sudden and unexpected change in roles that happens at the end of the story of Esther. Those who sought to attack the Jews were put on the defensive. Haman was hanged on the very same gallows he

---

[1] Esther 6:9.

prepared for Mordecai. The would-be Jewish victims became the victors. While I loved the holiday, I wondered why it was named after the Persian word for "lots," *pur*. I knew that Haman cast lots to choose the date for the annihilation of the Jews, but this seemed like a trivial detail hardly worth mentioning.

When I was researching the Scroll of Esther, I also read about ancient pagan superstitions and saw how central casting lots was to the message. The date chosen by lots wasn't random happenstance to Haman. In his pagan worldview, the lots revealed one of the greatest powers in the Universe, the power of "fate." The ancient pagans believed that everything in the Universe was subject to fate, even the gods. By casting the *pur*, Haman believed he was sealing the fate of the Jews. Naming the festival "Purim" was a way of mocking this belief and proclaiming that the God of Israel controls everything, not fate. Calling the festival Purim reminds us that the series of seemingly random events that a pagan would attribute to fate was actually the God of Israel intervening in history to save His people. The pagan lots were powerless against the infinite power of the one true God.

Mordecai alluded to God's role in saving the Jews in a central scene in which he asked Esther to convince her husband, the king, to rescind Haman's evil decree. Esther sent back word that she couldn't go before the king without an invitation. Persian law dictated that anyone who came into the royal court uninvited was to be executed and this even applied to the queen. The only way to avoid certain death would be for the king to extend his scepter when Esther approached. She doubted that her husband would extend his scepter if she appeared uninvited; he had not summoned her for thirty days. At this point, Mordechai responded to Esther with what is arguably the central message of the entire book:

> Do not think in your heart that you will escape in the king's palace any more than all the other Jews. For if you indeed remain silent at this time, *relief and salvation shall arise for the Jews from another place*, but you and your father's house will be

> destroyed. And who knows if for a time such as this you have attained royalty.[1]

The message here is that God caused the events that made Esther queen, thus placing her in a position to save the Jews, just as He caused the events that made Joseph viceroy, thereby putting him in a position to save his brothers. While God is in control, executing His plan by influencing events from behind the scenes, there is also free will. God doesn't force anyone to do anything. If Esther refused to play her role, God would have saved His people through some other means. But she would have perished for her failure to do the right thing. This was what Mordecai meant when he said, "relief and salvation shall arise for the Jews from another place." That other "place" was some other series of divinely influenced events that would have brought about the salvation of the Jews from Haman's genocidal plot.

As I was studying God's apparent absence from the Scroll of Esther, I realized it mirrored His apparent absence from the events themselves. Although God is not expressly mentioned anywhere in the scroll, His influence is felt through the series of perfectly timed events that bring about the Jews' salvation. God appears to be missing from the scroll and the events precisely because He is acting from behind the scenes. He never puts His word in the mouth of one of His prophets or sends down a pillar of cloud to protect His people. Instead, He influences numerous events to execute His plan. Any one of these events by itself could be explained away as a coincidence. However, the sum total of the events and their outcome are proof of God's protection.

God is obvious in these events even though He is not expressly mentioned anywhere in the story. God is effectively hidden in plain sight. The name Esther itself alludes to God hidden in these events. Her real name was Hadassah and she was given the name Esther to hide her identity. Any Persian would assume her name referred to their version of the pagan fertility goddess "Ishtar." However, in

---

[1] Esther 4:13–14.

Hebrew, Esther means, "hidden." Her name refers to her hidden identity as well as to God's hidden role in the events. God foiled Haman's diabolical conspiracy with His *hester panim*, "hidden face."

Learning about God's hidden face in the Scroll of Esther, I suddenly realized what the priests were talking about for all those years when they blessed us with the words, "May Yehovah lift His face towards you."[1] God lifting His face towards us was the opposite of Him hiding His face from us. Instead of acting from behind the scenes with *hester panim*, this part of the blessing was about God performing overt miracles in our lives. This doesn't necessarily mean sending a pillar of cloud. The intervention in Joseph's life was primarily through the "hidden face" but there were also some overt miracles in the form of dreams and Joseph's ability to interpret them.

I was taught with my Litvak upbringing that only the superstitious masses saw any importance in dreams. However, when it came to the story of Joseph, my teachers had to admit God's supernatural intervention. Joseph himself says, "the interpretation [of dreams] belongs to God" so not even a Litvak could disregard God's role.[2] The dreams in Joseph's life were not a "behind-the-scenes" God-incidence but the *overt* intervention of God. The rabbis call this type of overt divine protection *gilui panim*, "revealed face," but I prefer to use the terminology of the Priestly Blessing and call it *neso panim*, God's "lifted face."

As I was studying the stories of Esther and Joseph, it occurred to me that what one person saw as God's *hidden face* might appear to another as God's *lifted face.* Still a third person, perhaps a Litvak, might look at the same events as purely random happenstance unrelated to God. I began to look for examples in the Bible where God's lifted face was revealed to some, but remained hidden to others. I immediately thought of one of my favorite stories in the Bible, about the prophet Elisha who was surrounded by the entire Syrian army. The prophet's servant was terrified and certain they

---

[1] Numbers 6:26.

[2] Genesis 40:8.

were done for. Elisha assured him, "Have no fear, there are more on our side than on theirs."

Elisha's servant must have thought that the prophet was delusional until suddenly he saw what Elisha was able to see all along:

> ...and he saw, behold, the mountains all around Elisha were full of horses and chariots of fire.[1]

Elisha prayed to God that the army of angels would strike the Syrians with temporary blindness so he could lead them into the hands of the army of Israel. When the Syrians regained their vision and found themselves surrounded by Israelites, I wonder if they chalked it up to a colossal coincidence. I could imagine the Syrian scientists coming up with complex explanations of how dust from a volcano thousands of miles away flew into the eyes of their soldiers, temporarily blinding them. Elisha and his servant knew better, that this was a divine miracle, God protecting them through *neso panim*, His "lifted face."

Another ancient miracle revealed to some but hidden from others took place during the reign of King Hezekiah who faced the invasion of Sennacherib, the King of Assyria in 701 BCE. When Sennacherib demanded his immediate surrender, Hezekiah responded that he would trust in the God of Israel who promised through the prophet Isaiah to protect him. The Assyrian king laughed at this response and warned Hezekiah that he was more powerful than the God of Israel.

"Who among all the gods of these nations," Sennacherib boasted, "has saved their land from my hand? Will Yehovah really save Jerusalem from my hand?"[2]

God responded to Sennacherib's blasphemy by sending an angel to wipe out the bulk of his army:

> And it came to pass that night that an angel of Yehovah went forth and struck 185,000 in the camp of Assyria, and

---

[1] 2 Kings 6:17.
[2] 2 Kings 18:35.

> they woke up in the morning and behold they were all dead corpses.[1]

I must admit that I used to have trouble believing this story. I was taught that angels were something for simpletons to believe, because they could not comprehend God's greatness in an intellectual way. Besides, the magnitude of this miracle made me wonder if it wasn't a simple allegory or parable. I first read this story when I was a teenager back in the 1980s—a time when the Soviet Union still threatened the world with global thermonuclear war. When I read about Sennacherib's army being wiped out by an angel, I thought of what this would look like in modern times. I imagined a swarm of Soviet tanks sweeping across Western Europe; then one morning a Soviet general finding all of his tanks full of "dead corpses." This didn't sound plausible to me. The God I was taught to believe in didn't do things like that. It was too obvious, too overt. I had a much easier time believing in the hidden miracles.

Years later, I found out that this example of God lifting His face towards Israel—protecting us from our enemies with an overt miracle—was one of the best documented in history. Like most ancient nations (and some modern ones), the Assyrians rarely reported their own military failures. However, the Greek historian Herodotus, who lived two hundred years after Sennacherib, confirms that the Assyrian army was wiped out.[2] Although Herodotus confused some of the details, he was clearly talking about the same events described in the Book of Kings. Herodotus attributed the Assyrian defeat to an invasion of field mice that overran the Assyrian army camp. Based on Herodotus's report, some modern secular historians argue that the Assyrians must have died from an epidemic like the Black Plague, spread by flea-infested rodents. I have no problem accepting this. It is completely consistent with the Bible, which attributes the death of the Assyrians to an angel. God accomplished most miracles in the Bible through some natural

---

[1] 2 Kings 19:35.

[2] Herodotus, *The History of Herodotus*, translated into English by G. C. Macaulay, book 2, section 141.

mechanism, which He caused to behave in a supernatural way. For example, when God brought the plague of locusts upon Egypt, the Bible says:

> …and Yehovah drove an east wind in the land all that day and all that night; in the morning the east wind had carried the locusts.[1]

Both wind and locusts are part of nature. What made it a miracle was that God caused the locusts to swarm and be blown into Egypt at that exact time.

In the case of the Assyrian army, the Bible tells us that God sent an angel to wipe them out but it does not tell us what natural mechanism the angel used. This wouldn't be the first time an angel used an epidemic to carry out God's wrath. In the Book of Samuel, David sinned against God who responded by punishing Israel with a plague. When the plague began spreading in Jerusalem, King David saw "the angel of Yehovah standing between the earth and the heaven with his sword drawn in his hand, stretched out over Jerusalem."[2]

Secular historians refuse to acknowledge that the epidemic in David's day was the work of an angel, just as they refuse to acknowledge the epidemic that struck the Assyrians was the work of an angel. As in the case of Elisha and his servant facing the Syrians, some people's eyes are closed to the cause of these miracles. It appears to them to be mere coincidence or random happenstance, with a perfectly naturalistic explanation. I believe the words of Scripture that tell of the destruction of the Assyrian army by God's angel but have no problem believing the angel used an infestation of field mice or some other natural mechanism to accomplish this.[3] This was God lifting His face towards Israel as sure as the plague of

---

[1] Exodus 10:13.

[2] 1 Chronicles 21:16.

[3] The specific mechanism may have been an outbreak of septicemic plague causing high fever and rapid death. This would explain why Isaiah (30:27–33) prophesied about God's destruction of the Assyrians using various metaphors related to fire including the burning of the *Topheth*, see below.

locusts in Egypt and the pillar of cloud in the desert, even if some people want to dismiss it as pure coincidence or dumb luck.

During the 1973 Yom Kippur War, Israel experienced a modern-day act of God's protection. To this day it is still a matter of dispute among the faithful as to whether this was God lifting His face through an overt miracle or hiding His face and influencing events from behind the scenes. The miracle took place on the Golan Heights—a historical part of the Land of Israel that extends across a twenty-mile-wide barren plateau. During nineteen years of Syrian occupation, the Jewish towns of the Jordan Valley and Western Galilee were terrorized by Syrian gunners high up on the western edge of the Golan, firing indiscriminately at civilian targets. This only ended after Israel liberated the Golan Heights in the 1967 Six Day War.

Then, on October 6, 1973, the Syrians launched an unprovoked surprise attack, storming into the Golan with a force of 1,400 tanks. They knew Israel relied on a citizen's army made up of reservists so they coordinated their attack with Egypt for Yom Kippur, the Day of Atonement. Most reserve soldiers were in the synagogues, weak from fasting and far from the front. Israel's standing army only had 177 tanks deployed on the Golan at the start of the war. The Israeli forward lines of defense quickly collapsed along most of the border.

By the second day of the war, Syrian units had penetrated to within a few miles of the strategic bridges over the Jordan River. From there, all of Israel lay before them virtually undefended. The Syrians could have barreled across the Jordan and put an end to the Jewish State. Instead, a miracle happened. Simon Dunstan, a military historian who wrote one of the definitive books on the war, explains:

> With their leading units within sight of the Sea of Galilee following their overwhelming triumph on the southern Golan, the Syrians inexplicably halted their offensive and the momentum was lost never to be regained.[1]

---

1 Simon Dunstan, *The Yom Kippur War*, Osprey 2007, page 4. Compare also, Abraham Rabinovich, *The Yom Kippur War*, Schocken Books 2005, page 195: "...the reason [the

No one knows for sure why the Syrians stopped. When I heard about this miracle, I began to devour a series of books on the battles that raged in the Golan Heights during the war. I learned that the Syrians struck across the border in a three-pronged attack, which was initially successful in the central and southern Golan but was held up in the north. All the books I read agreed that the Syrians should have poured their forces into the central and southern districts, seizing the bridges over the Jordan River before Israel had a chance to mobilize. Instead, the central and southern prongs of the attack seemed to be waiting for the northern prong to catch up. The northern prong, for its part, got bogged down in one of the fiercest tank battles in history in a place that would come to be known as the "Valley of Tears."

"Fascinating!" I exclaimed in my Spock voice. I had to go see this for myself.

I left Jerusalem at 4:30 a.m. and headed for the Golan. The drive north took about two and a half hours and I arrived in the cool of the morning, before the heat of the July sun began to bake the black volcanic basalt rock that covers the Golan Heights. On my way to the Valley of Tears, I drove by a bunch of old tanks lined up on a ridge and decided to stop and investigate. It was a war memorial honoring the fallen soldiers of the 7th Armored Brigade. These were the Israelis who stopped the Syrians in the decisive battle I was coming to learn about. I looked around at the old Israeli tanks and then noticed a large inscription alongside the brigade insignia. The inscription was a verse from the Book of Isaiah that said, "Behold Yehovah, He comes with fire, and like a tempest His chariots."[1] The armored brigade that defeated the Syrians recognized that the God of Israel was fighting alongside them! I took this to be the first witness that I was dealing with a miracle.

I continued on my way to the Valley of Tears and eventually reached another war memorial that honored the fallen soldiers of the 77th Battalion of the 7th Armored Brigade. This was the tank battalion that held off the Syrians in the Valley of Tears. I did not realize until

---

Syrians] did not continue their attack at night after breaking through in the southern Golan is one of the major remaining mysteries of the war."

[1] Isaiah 66:15.

I arrived at the second memorial that it was located on the very spot that the Israeli defenders held during the battle. At the center of the memorial was a destroyed Syrian tank that penetrated the Israeli lines. Its burned-out hull was all that remained—a reminder of just how desperate the battle had been.

I remembered a story from the book *The Heights of Courage* by Avigdor Kahalani, the Israeli tank commander in charge of the 77th battalion. On the first night of the battle, Kahalani looked over at the tanks under his command and—to his horror—saw that one of them had a red brake light on. He yelled over the radio ordering the offending tank to turn off the light quickly before the Syrians spotted it. The response came back that all the lights were off. Kahalani peeked out of his turret and was annoyed to find the red light still on. He contacted each tank, one at a time, and all denied having any lights on. Kahalani then ordered all of his tanks to kill their engines. Looking through a pair of binoculars, he could make out a plume of black engine exhaust silhouetted against the red brake light. The engine of the offending tank was still on and Kahalani swallowed hard as he realized what this meant. A Syrian tank had infiltrated his ranks.

By this point Kahalani felt helpless. The Syrians had a huge tactical advantage in the form of the latest Soviet night-vision equipment. In contrast, the Israelis were essentially blind at night. All the Israelis possessed were high-powered floodlights mounted atop their tanks, but using them would reveal their position to the enemy. He had no choice: Kahalani ordered his men to load a shell and aim directly for the glowing red light. He then ordered another tank to prepare to shine its floodlight at the suspect tank. He needed to be sure he wasn't firing on a friendly tank, maybe one with a broken radio that had not heard his order to turn off the light. The floodlight illuminated the target. It was a Soviet-made T-55, a Syrian tank. It was only 50 yards away.

"Fire!" Kahalani yelled at his gunner.

The enemy tank burst into flames from the impact of the Israeli shell.[1]

Now I was standing in front of the burned out hull of a Syrian tank, maybe the one Kahalani destroyed that night. This was definitely a sign of how desperate the Israeli situation was during that battle. The Israeli victory was nothing short of a miracle.

As I walked around the war memorial that had once been a battlefield, I came across the insignia of Kahalani's 77th Battalion. At the center of the insignia was a tank. Across the top were the colors of the Israeli flag, an olive branch representing peace, and three flaming arrows. What caught my attention was the single Hebrew word emblazoned at the bottom of the insignia, right below the tank. It read *Oz*, as in *Migdal Oz*, "strong Tower." In Hebrew, each letter has a numerical value and the word *Oz* adds up to 77, the designation of the battalion that defeated the Syrians. Here was my second witness. The King had extended His scepter, inviting me to believe.

When I saw the battalion insignia, I felt bad for the Syrians. They did not realize they were sending the northern component of their invasion force against a battalion that bore testimony to the *Migdal Oz*—the Strong Tower—of God's powerful name. Still, the Syrians must have thought that driving only three miles through the two-mile-wide valley would be easy. They had 500 tanks and hundreds of other armored fighting vehicles in the northern Golan alone. The Israelis were outnumbered fifteen-to-one at the start of the battle. They deployed along the "line of hills," a series of volcanic cones overlooking the Valley of Tears, and they began to open fire on the relentless Syrian onslaught.

In his book, Kahalani describes how his men were dying to his left and to his right as the Syrians pressed forward for four grueling days. He knew he had to continue to fight because of the "existential" nature of this war. If the Syrians lost, they would be humiliated; if Israel lost, it would cease to exist. As one Israeli tank commander would later explain, they were fighting to stop the

---

[1] Avigdor Kahalani, *The Heights of Courage*, Kindle edition, pages 50–52.

"Second Holocaust."[1] Despite the huge imbalance of numbers, Kahalani's small and desperate force managed to inflict staggering losses on the Syrians. By the end of the fourth day, they destroyed some 260 Syrian tanks along with hundreds of armored personnel carriers and other enemy vehicles.[2]

The series of events that led to this victory rivals anything in the life of Joseph or Esther. Perhaps the single most miraculous event was the arrival of vital reinforcements at a moment when Kahalani was down to only seven tanks, almost out of ammunition and fuel, and had lost control of the "line of hills" that dominated the Valley of Tears. The reinforcements were headed by Yosi Ben-Chanan, a tank commander who was on his honeymoon in Nepal when the war broke out. He arranged to take a series of flights through Teheran and Athens in order to get back and defend Israel. His family was waiting for him at the airport with his uniform. He immediately drove to the northern front where he managed to cobble together a force of thirteen tanks, damaged in earlier fighting but now patched together, barely battleworthy. He then scraped together ad hoc tank crews made up of reservists and wounded soldiers who "escaped" from the hospital to return to the fray. Ben-Chanan's hodge-podge force seized the line of hills overlooking the Valley of Tears just as Kahalani fired his last rounds at the Syrians. Not long thereafter, the Syrians began to retreat.

So, why did the Syrians retreat? After the war, Kahalani's commander, Yanush Ben-Gal, offered his own explanation:

> The Syrians, apparently, assumed that they had no chance of success. They did not know the truth, that our situation was desperate.[3]

Anyone who thinks that the Syrians were cowards that ran at the first sign of trouble should read Kahalani's book.

---

[1] Tzvika Greengold, *Tzvika Force*, Modan Publishing House Ltd., page 113 [Hebrew].

[2] Chaim Herzog, *The War of Atonement*, Casemate 1975, page 113.

[3] Simon Dunstan, *The Yom Kippur War*, Osprey 2007, page 173.

"The Syrians were still coming," Kahalani writes, "and the fact that the damage to their comrades didn't stop them was worrying me. Could they be that brave? Hard to believe."[1]

This was the second day of the invasion and the Syrians continued to try breaking through the Valley of Tears for two more days. The Syrian determination and bravery was impressive but not as impressive as the Israeli *audacity* to come against a force fifteen times their size. What gave Kahalani and his men the resolve to hold the Syrians back through nearly eighty grueling hours of battle? What gave Ben-Chanan the *chutzpah* to show up with thirteen damaged tanks manned by wounded soldiers to stand up to the Syrian bullies?

Many Israelis insist that this was nothing less than God lifting His face towards Israel, performing an overt miracle to save His people from annihilation. The Israeli documentary *Zero Hour* describes this miracle in the words of a captured Syrian officer interrogated by Israeli intelligence after the war. According to the documentary, the intelligence officer asked the Syrian, "What is the reason you stopped on the line of hills on the Golan Heights?" The Syrian responded:

> I would like to see you cross the Syrian line of hills when you see a whole row of white angels standing above the line of hills and a white hand from the heavens signaling to you, "Stop!" I stopped![2]

I have to admit that every time I hear this story I am overcome with emotion. At the same time, when it comes to the appearance of angels, I'm like Agent Mulder in *The X-Files*, "I want to believe!"[3]

As if the Syrian retreat was not enough, the next part of the story is no less miraculous. Kahalani's seven surviving tanks joined Ben-Chanan's patched-up thirteen and started to *pursue* the retreating Syrians who still had hundreds of undamaged tanks in the field.[4] This

---

[1] Avigdor Kahalani, *The Heights of Courage*, Kindle edition, page 67.

[2] *Shaat HaEfes (Zero Hour)*, published at http://www.hidabroot.org/MediaDetail.asp?MediaID=887 [Hebrew].

[3] *The X-Files*, created by Chris Carter, 1993–2002.

[4] Jerry Asher and Eric Hammel, *Duel for the Golan*, Pacifica Military 1987, Kindle edition, chapter 22; Chaim Herzog, *The War of Atonement*, Casemate 1975, page 113.

trumps angels in my view! It's a literal fulfillment of the blessing promised to Israel in Leviticus:

> Five of you will chase a hundred and a hundred will chase ten thousand, and your enemies will fall before you by the sword.[1]

The blessing promised in Deuteronomy elaborates upon this theme:

> Yehovah will cause your enemies who rise up against you to be defeated before your face… and all the people of the earth will see that *the name of Yehovah is proclaimed over you* and they will fear you.[2]

Shortly before the Syrian invasion began, *kohanim* across the land recited the Priestly Blessing as part of the prayer service for the Day of Atonement. Back in 1973, most Aaronic priests adhered to tradition, substituting the Tetragrammaton with Adonai (Lord). Nevertheless, they still placed Yehovah's holy name over the people using their secret hand cipher, the one the Jewish actor who played Spock adopted for his Vulcan greeting. God honored their intention as promised in the 44th chapter of Psalms, "If we forgot the name of our God… God would surely search it out, for He knows the secrets of the heart."[3]

Whether it was a row of angels or a series of perfectly timed events, the Israeli victory in the Yom Kippur War was a miracle. It doesn't really matter if God lifted His face towards Israel or hid His face, whether it was an overt miracle or a hidden one, it was a miracle of Biblical proportions. If God performed such a great miracle with a substitute, what would happen if the *kohanim* started actually speaking His holy name as He commanded them to do in the Book of Numbers?

The more I studied the battles on the Golan Heights, the more I became convinced that this was an example of modern-day Esther-protection with divine intervention hidden in plain sight. The

---

[1] Leviticus 26:8.

[2] Deuteronomy 28:7, 10.

[3] Psalms 44:20–21[21–22].

numbers I kept coming across demonstrated this. As a natural skeptic, numbers do not impress me easily. However, when I learned that the main Syrian force in the Valley of Tears was the 7th Division, I couldn't ignore them anymore. When I put all the information together, the hand of God became manifest. It turned out that the 7th Syrian Division launched a surprise attack in the 7th Hebrew month on the 7th day of the week and was stopped by 7 surviving tanks from the 77th Battalion of the 7th Israeli Armored Brigade after about 77 hours of battle. Someone say, "God-incidence!"

In the 20th chapter of Psalms, King David explains what set apart his army from that of his enemies:

> They call on chariots, they call on horses, but *we call on the name of Yehovah* our God. They bowed down and fell, but we rose and stood up.[1]

Like King David, Israel's 7th Armored Brigade called on the name of our God proclaiming, "Behold Yehovah, He comes with fire, and like a tempest His chariots." The Syrians came face-to-face with the *migdal oz*, the "strong tower" of Yehovah's mighty name. They certainly had the advantage of surprise, technology, and numbers but they had no idea they were facing two armies: one with chariots of steel and another with chariots of fire. We won because, as Elisha said to his servant when he faced the Syrians of his day, "there were more with us than with them."

When I face the figurative Syrians in my life, I know that the God of Israel is stronger than any armor and more powerful than any tanks. I trust in Him to give me the *audacity* to deal with difficult situations where the numbers are against me. I pray that He gives me the *resolve* of Kahalani and the *chutzpah* of Ben-Chanan to stand up to the circumstances that relentlessly press against me. I ask Him to fulfill the Priestly Blessing in my life, whether with a pillar of cloud or through a series of perfectly timed God-incidences, with His face hidden or revealed.

---

[1] Psalms 20:7–8[8–9].

Chapter 12:

To Hell and Back

The deep gully filled with the melodic sound of flutes and the rhythmic beating of drums. The young father felt the heat of the fire crackling up from the deep pit, licking the insides of the hollow reddish-brown statue. He clutched the naked body of his screaming infant, knowing what was coming next. He tried desperately not to cry but paternal instinct kicked in, sending a tear down his cheek. Then the priest wrenched the baby out of his hands and placed it into the arms of the idol. By now, the metal god was glowing red-hot and its bronze embrace instantly seared the soft skin of the innocent child. The music grew louder, ferociously trying to drown out the blood-curdling cries of the sacrificial victim. Finally, the heat caused the baby's body to shrivel up and fall down into the fire-pit.

I was in Hell. Literally. The valley on the outskirts of ancient Jerusalem that gave Hell its name. In ancient times, the sinful Jews of Jerusalem sacrificed their children here to the Ammonite deity, Molech. God warned the Israelites in the desert that He considered human sacrifice to be an abomination, but King Solomon's Ammonite wife convinced him to build the *Topheth*, an altar for sacrificing children to Molech.

The cult of Molech was so horrific that it left its imprint on the collective consciousness of the Jewish People as a symbol of the worst suffering imaginable. Isaiah used this symbolism to describe the great devastation that God would visit upon the King of Assyria, who was demanding Hezekiah's surrender:

> The Topheth is already prepared, it is made ready for the king, it is prepared deep and wide; its pit with an abundance

> of fire and wood, the breath of Yehovah kindles it like a stream of sulfur.[1]

When later Jews wanted to paint a picture of the punishment of the wicked on the Day of Judgment, they described it as the suffering of the "Hinnom Valley," the deep gorge outside Jerusalem where the Topheth was located. In Hebrew, it was called *Ge-Hinnom* (Valley of Hinnom), in Greek *Gehenna*, and in English translated as "Hell."[2]

I came to Hell, the place of the Topheth in the Hinnom Valley because of something a Christian tourist once said to me. She was a little old Southern lady I met many years ago in Jerusalem.

"You're goin' to Hell!" she announced with a thick southern drawl. "The Jews are going to burn in Hell," she continued, "because they have no grace." She went on to explain that unless I accepted Jesus as my Lord and Savior, I was destined for the "pit of Hell."

Sometimes people say things without thinking about what their words really mean. I came to the valley that gave Hell its name to consider the true significance of what this woman was saying. If the Hinnom Valley was the symbol of the punishment in store for me, I wanted to understand what that meant. But how could I comprehend the horror of child sacrifice? I'm not sure what I expected to find here. There was nothing in my modern-day experience that could compare to the burning of innocent children. *Or was there?*

The next morning, I headed over to Yad Vashem, Israel's national Holocaust museum located at the edge of the Jerusalem Forest. I came to see the Children's Memorial, built to commemorate the 1.5 million Jewish children murdered by the Nazis. The memorial consists of a round subterranean chamber illuminated by the

---

[1] Isaiah 30:33. The "fire" mentioned throughout this prophecy may allude to fever caused by the rodent-borne plague that wiped out the Assyrian army, see above.

[2] The Hebrew *Ge-Hinnom* (sometimes *Ge-Ben-Hinnom*) appears thirteen times in the Hebrew Bible: Joshua 15:8 (twice); 18:16 (twice); 2 Kings 23:10; Jeremiah 7:31, 32; 19:2, 6; 32:35; Nehemiah 11:30; 2 Chronicles 28:3; 33:6. It also appears four times in the *Mishnah* (Eduyot 2:10; Ethics of the Fathers 1:5; 5:19, 20) and fourteen times in the Aramaic *Targum Jonathan* (1 Samuel 2:8, 9 [twice]; Isaiah 26:15, 19; 30:33; 33:14, 17; 53:9; 65:5; 66:24; Jeremiah 17:13; Hosea 14:9[10]; Nahum 1:8). The Greek *Gehenna* appears twelve times in the New Testament: Matthew 5:22, 29, 30; 10:28; 18:9; 23:15, 33; Mark 9:43, 45, 47; Luke 12:5; James 3:6.

flickering light of dozens of candles. In Jewish tradition, a candle is lit to remind us of a deceased loved one, usually on the anniversary of their passing. The light of the candles at the Children's Memorial is reflected by a myriad of mirrors. As you walk around the room, the number of candles seems constantly to increase as the light bounces off the mirrors from different angles. It gives the impression that there were more children murdered than a normal person could possibly count. The effect is amplified further by the calm voice of a woman over a loudspeaker calling out the name of each child, how old they were when they were murdered, and their country of origin. *Sara Horovitz, 3 years old, Poland; Jacob Dondorp, 12 years old, Holland; Miryam Echkenazy, 6 years old, Greece.* The effect is powerful. It conveys the magnitude of the crime by individualizing the victims. You realize that each one of the countless candles represents another Sara, another Jacob, another Miryam—another child whom the Nazis murdered. It was a modern-day Molech but on a grand scale.

The Children's Memorial gave me some perspective on what the little old Christian lady was talking about. She told me that I was going to Hell for believing what God revealed to Moses and for doing my best to obey what all the prophets of the Old Testament preached. As a Jew, I would receive *no grace* from God. The God she portrayed was ruthless, merciless, and heartless. Like a priest of Molech who burned the children in the Valley of Hinnom. Like the SS monsters who shot, starved, gassed, and incinerated an entire generation.

I sensed in the little old Christian lady's words what I call the "*spirit* of Marcionism." Marcion was a 2nd Century Christian bishop born at Sinope on the southern shore of the Black Sea. He believed that the God of the Old Testament and the God of the New Testament were two different Gods. Marcion taught that the God of the Old Testament was a God of *hate* whereas the God of the New Testament was a God of *love*. The God of the Old Testament was a God of *vengeance* whereas the God of the New Testament was a God of *forgiveness*. The God of the Old Testament was a God of *cruelty* whereas the God of the New Testament was a God of *mercy*.

Mainstream Christianity branded Marcion a heretic, but some of his *spirit* survives today.

I experienced a taste of Marcionism when Keith Johnson sent the book we wrote together to an evangelical scholar whom he knew. He assumed the evangelical scholar would love a book that explores the Jewish background of Christianity while still honoring its sacred texts.

At one point in the book, we quoted a rabbi we met at a beach on the Sea of Galilee. The little old rabbi told us he believed that when Christians worship God as "Father" they are worshipping the same God as the Jews. Keith's evangelical scholar went ballistic when he read this and furiously scribbled into the margin of the book, "No! The Christian God is △!" He then sent the book back to Keith via registered mail to show his disdain and dissatisfaction.

I found it ironic that the evangelical scholar chose a triangle to symbolize the nature of his Christian God as distinct from the Jewish God. Jewish mystics use the very same symbol to express the eternal nature of our God who is described by the three Hebrew verbs *hayah*, *hoveh*, and *yihyeh*—"He was," "He is," and "He will be." This description of God is proclaimed publicly in traditional Jewish synagogue services every Sabbath in the *Adon Olam* prayer. Because the name Yehovah is actually a combination of *hayah*, *hoveh*, and *yihye*, it could be legitimately translated as, "He who was, He who is, and He who will be." According to some Jews, one of the triangles that form the Star of David represents these three Hebrews verbs and hence the infinite and eternal nature of God. The other triangle represents King David and hence his descendant the Messiah.[1] In the true spirit of Marcionism, the evangelical scholar was saying, "Our Christian triangle is better than your Jewish triangle." The little old lady was taking this one step further, painting the God of the Jewish Bible as a cruel and ruthless deity who condemns His people to hellfire for doing their best to obey what He taught them through His prophets.

---

[1] The second triangle, according to this theory, represents David whose name is written with the Hebrew letter *dalet*, shaped like a triangle in Paleo-Hebrew.

I was troubled by what the little old Christian lady said until I went back to Hell. It was the day after my visit to Yad Vashem and I needed to take care of some unfinished business. On my earlier visit, I encountered a bone lying out in a field not far from where the priests of Molech once performed their monstrous rituals. The bone was covered in many layers of fossilized moss, which I knew from my archaeology days meant it had laid there for millennia. It was a small bone, probably the femur of a child, and I wondered if it had not come from one of those sacrificial victims. When I first saw it, I was freaked out and stared at it for a few minutes before walking away. Then for two days, I couldn't stop thinking about the bone of this innocent youth.

Jewish tradition considers it a sacrilege to leave a body unburied. This goes back to a verse in Deuteronomy, which states that a person who is executed must be buried by sunset, because it is a curse to leave a body exposed. The Jewish thinking is that if a murderer deserves to have his body buried, then surely the innocent do as well. I remember learning as a child that one of the greatest acts of righteousness is *met mitzvah*—if you find the body of a stranger out on a country road, you must bury it. The rabbis teach that even a *kohen*, an Aaronic priest whom the Torah forbids from touching a dead body, must make an exception and bury a stranger who has no one else to care for his remains. I felt horrible that I saw the bone of this child lying unburied in the countryside and walked away without doing anything. I needed to go back and put this ancient victim to rest.

On my way back to Hell, I walked past "Bible Hill," which received its name for being the only hilltop in Jerusalem that remains pristine, looking today very much as it did in Biblical times. I remembered that on the other side of Bible Hill was the ancient tomb where archaeologists found the two silver scrolls containing the Priestly Blessing. Those were the same silver scrolls I saw years earlier in the Israel Museum, the ones inscribed with the name of Yehovah in Paleo-Hebrew.

I was thinking about what the little old Christian lady said, that the Jews have "no grace." As I walked past Bible Hill, it occurred to me that the Priestly Blessing inscribed on those two silver scrolls, the oldest surviving copy of any Biblical text, proved she was wrong. Part of the blessing says, "May Yehovah… be gracious to you."[1] It was crystal clear to me that the God of the Hebrew Scriptures did have *grace* and even promised it in the blessing He taught the Aaronic priests to proclaim over His people.

With these thoughts racing through my head, I hurried down into the Hinnom Valley to recover the bone of the child victim. When I finally found it, I hiked up to the top of Bible Hill. I laid the bone to rest under a pile of twelve stones, not far from the ancient burial cave in which the silver scrolls with the Priestly Blessing were discovered.

Looking out over that sacred landscape, I realized it immortalized a profound contrast between grace and cruelty, between truth and falsehood, between good and evil. Bible Hill where the silver scrolls were found testifies to the benevolence of the God of Israel who blesses His people with grace. Not far away, the Hinnom Valley, where the Topheth was located, testifies to the cruelty and indifference of the god of the Ammonites who consumed his devotees, sending their charred corpses literally down into the fiery pit of Hell.

What an amazing picture! How could the little old Christian lady say the Hebrew God had no grace for His people? She was saying that God was no longer in a covenant relationship with Israel. This is contrary to what Jeremiah prophesied:

> Thus says Yehovah, who gives the sun to light the day and the statutes of the moon and stars to light the night… If these statutes depart from before Me, says Yehovah, so too shall the seed of Israel cease from being a nation in My presence all the days.[2]

The very appearance of the sun, moon, and stars in the sky testifies to God's continuing relationship with the People of Israel who He

---

[1] Numbers 6:25.
[2] Jeremiah 31:35–36.

blessed with grace. This is the same God who proclaimed to a sinful nation:

> For I am Yehovah, I do not change; therefore, you are not consumed, O sons of Jacob.[1]

If God were to change, He would consume us in a heartbeat, but He continues to honor His covenant and extend grace to His undeserving people. I started to wonder if the little old Christian lady had a different understanding of the concept of "grace" than what I was seeing throughout the Hebrew Bible. Perhaps we were talking about two different things. I needed to go back to the sources and define "grace."

I started with the Priestly Blessing. The five English words, "and be gracious to you" are the translation of a single Hebrew word: *vee-choo-ne-ka*. I knew the source of this tongue twister was the Hebrew noun *chen*, usually translated into English as "grace." When the *kohanim* bless the people with the word *vee-choo-ne-ka*, they are really saying, "[may Yehovah] have *chen* towards you" or "[may Yehovah] treat you with *chen*." So, what is *chen*?

I wanted to get past my own preconceptions so I pulled out three dictionaries of ancient Hebrew and started to look up dozens of verses that use the word in different ways. I found out there are five main meanings of the Hebrew word for "grace," each revolving around a single idea.

The literal meaning of *chen* can be found in a small number of verses that speak about a precious gem having *chen* or a crown having *chen*.[2] In these literal contexts, *chen* describes the "sparkle" of the gem or the "gleam" of the precious metal from which the crown is made. So the Hebrew word for "grace" literally means the *sparkle* or *gleam* of a precious metal or gem.

---

[1] Malachi 3:6 [adapted from NKJV].

[2] Proverbs 17:8 literally says, "A bribe is a sparkling stone to its owner," meaning the bribe serves to entice like a diamond or a precious gem. Proverbs 4:9 compares "wisdom" to an "ornament of grace" [KJV] but literally in Hebrew a "gleaming crown" (*livyat chen*).

From this literal meaning, we get *chen*/ grace in the sense of "favor." This is the meaning of, "he/ she found *favor* in his eyes," an expression used no less than forty-nine times in the Hebrew Bible. This phrase describes any relationship that elicits feelings of love and compassion such as a woman finding favor in the eyes of her husband.[1] Although *chen* means "favor" in this context, the literal meaning is not lost. *Chen* is the *sparkle* in the eyes of the husband, looking with love and compassion towards his wife.

I was curious why a *sparkling* eye would be associated with love, so I called up my youngest sister, a Jerusalem-based optometrist, and asked her for a physiological explanation. She told me that when we see a "sparkle" or "twinkle" in someone's eye, it is caused by tears welling up in the eyes along with dilation of the pupils. These are both involuntary physiological responses to strong emotion. The tears and dilated pupils reflect an increased amount of light that we perceive as a twinkle in the eye.

While most people may not realize why an eye twinkles, we subconsciously know that it expresses a strong, positive emotion. When we look up at God and "find favor in His eyes," our heavenly Father's paternal instinct kicks in, metaphorically causing His pupils to dilate and tears to well up in His eyes as He looks down on us. God's *chen*—His *favor*—is the sparkle in His eyes that expresses His love and compassion for His children.

The third usage of *chen* is as a verb, meaning "to give a gift." The Bible says that when Esau met his long lost brother Jacob after not seeing him for many years he asked who all the children were traveling with him. Jacob responded:

> [These are] the children with which God *chen*-ed me.[2]

God *chen*-ing—gracing—Jacob with children means He looked at Jacob with a sparkle in His eye and gave him the gift of children. Similarly, the Psalmist prays:

> *Chen* me with Your Torah.[1]

---

[1] Deuteronomy 24:1; Esther 8:5.

[2] Genesis 33:5.

The Psalmist is asking God to grace him with the gift of His perfect Word. The gift is given because of the love and compassion God feels when He looks at us.

By definition, a gift is "free," which is also the fourth meaning of *chen*, especially when used in the adverbial form, *chinam*. To do something *chinam* means to do it for free, without any charge or payment. In a literal sense, it means to do it out of love and compassion and not out of obligation.

The fifth meaning of *chen* is "mercy." This usage appears in the 34th chapter of Exodus in what I believe to be among the most important passages in the entire Bible. The section opens with Moses asking God to reveal His nature to him. God responds by proclaiming to Moses what are known as His *midot*—his behavioral characteristics. This passage is so important that it is paraphrased no less than *seven* times in the Bible and recited in traditional Jewish prayers on the high holidays:

> And Yehovah passed in front of his face and called out, "Yehovah, Yehovah, a God merciful (*rachum*) and gracious (*chanun*), long-suffering, full of true righteousness. He rewards righteousness to the thousandth generation, forgiving iniquity, transgression and sin."[2]

In this passage, God is said to be *chanun*, which means imbued with the characteristic of *chen*—grace. In plain English, it means God is *chen*-ful, "full of grace." By His very nature, God has that sparkle in His eyes when He looks at us. His grace in this context is manifested as "compassion." The associated divine characteristic *rachum* means, "mercy." The word *rachum* comes from a literal root meaning "womb" and expresses the feelings a woman instinctively has for the fruit of her womb—her children. God describing Himself as having the characteristics of the *womb* and the *sparkling eye* is another way of saying He is *merciful* and *compassionate*. This same usage appears in the prayer of the Psalmist in the verse:

---

[1] Psalms 119:29.

[2] Exodus 34:6–7. The verse is quoted or paraphrased in Joel 2:13; Jonah 4:2; Psalms 78:38; 86:15; 103:8; 145:8; Nehemiah 9:17.

> I have implored You with all my heart; have *chen*—compassion—towards me, in accordance with Your promise.[1]

Here, God's *chen*—His compassion—goes back to the covenant-promise He made with Israel. The sparkle is caused by the metaphorical tears welling up in God's eyes, reflecting the light of the sun, moon, and stars, which testify in the sky to His continuing relationship with Israel. The prophet Amos speaks about God's *chen* in this sense in the verse:

> Hate evil, love good; establish justice in the gate. It may be that Yehovah God of hosts will have *chen* for the remnant of Joseph.[2]

The prophet is calling upon Israel to repent, hoping that God will have *chen*—compassion—towards the sinful nation. The other meanings of *chen* are also implied here. Amos is saying that we cannot earn God's *forgiveness*, but we should repent anyway and hope for His *compassion*, which is a *free gift.* If He is gracious to us, it will not be because we deserve it but because of that *sparkle* He has in His eyes when He looks at us with *love and compassion.*

One of the greatest expressions of God's grace is His willingness to accept our repentance even though we may not deserve His forgiveness. In Hebrew, the word for repentance is *teshuvah*, which literally means, "return." After God proclaims in the Book of Malachi that He does not change, He goes on to promise His people:

> *Return* to Me and I will *return* to you.[3]

If we return to God in repentance, He will look at us with that sparkle in His eye and extend us His grace. God explains the reason for this in the Book of Ezekiel:

---

[1] Psalms 119:58 [adapted from NJPS].
[2] Amos 5:15 [adapted from NKJV].
[3] Malachi 3:7 [NKJV].

> Do I indeed desire the death of an evildoer, says Lord Yehovah? Do I not desire that he *return* from his ways and live?[1]

God is not sitting up in heaven waiting for us to mess up so He can cast us down into the pit of Hell. He wants us to return to Him in repentance so He can extend His *chen* and be compassionate towards us. He is constantly looking at us with a sparkle in His eyes, out of His love, wanting us to live.

God is so full of grace that He is even willing to help us return to Him in repentance. Jeremiah prayed for this kind of *chen* for Israel at the end of Lamentations:

> Return us to You, O Yehovah, and we will return.[2]

Jeremiah recognized that we cannot do it on our own, that we need God to help us return to Him. Of course, this is a two-way street because we must be willing to return, but we could never do it without His *gracious* help.

Reading about God's willingness to return us to Him reminded me of my visit to Ellis Island a year earlier. It was the same day I went to visit Ground Zero. While waiting all day for a flight back to Israel, I decided to do the tourist thing and visit the museum that now covers Ellis Island. I knew it was the port of entry for millions of Jewish refugees fleeing persecution in Eastern Europe, but I didn't think any of my ancestors came through there. I hoped that I might learn something about their experiences at other ports of entry.

After taking the ferry over from Battery Park, I spent a couple of hours making my way around the museum that now occupies the building where millions of immigrants were processed. In one corner of the museum, I came across a computer lab. The woman at the counter explained that for five dollars I could search their database for relatives that may have come through Ellis Island. I still had half a day before I needed to return to the airport, so I decided to shell out the five bucks.

---

[1] Ezekiel 18:23.
[2] Lamentations 5:21. See also Jeremiah 31:18.

"Who knows," I thought, "maybe I'll find a distant relative."

I did a few searches for various names, but found nothing. Then I decided to search for the man I'm named after, my great-grandfather, Nehemia Robinson. I knew that he fled Lithuania in the 1920s, dreaming of the Land of Israel. The British had conquered Israel from the Turks and imposed strict limits on Jewish immigration. With entry to Israel denied him, his second choice was the "goldene medina," America, where the streets were paved with gold. He had no idea how he'd get to America until one day he was contacted by a synagogue in Chicago in desperate need of an Orthodox rabbi. He spent the rest of his life as a rabbi on the West Side and never made it to the Promised Land.

My initial computer search for my great-grandfather didn't uncover anything, but then I tried a few spelling variations. To my surprise, I found his name. I went to the lady at the counter and asked her, "Now what?"

She came over to the computer, took the mouse, and clicked on a few links. A scan of an old type-written page came up on the screen. It was a ship's manifest. My great-grandfather's name was on line 15. I stared at the name: "Nechemja-Jakob Rubinson." The spelling was strange, but I knew to expect this. A few years earlier, I visited his grave and saw his name spelled "Nachemie Robinson." It was different from the spelling in the book he wrote on Talmudic law, which had "N. Rubinson." Every time the Americans tried to write his Hebrew name in English, it came out differently.

Still, I wanted to be sure this was really my great-grandfather. I carefully examined the page from the ship's manifest. I found out Nechemja-Jakob Rubinson arrived at Ellis Island on June 15, 1923 on the S.S. Mauretania. It listed him as a 46-year-old rabbi from "Wilno." I knew this was the Polish spelling of Vilna, the largest city in Lithuania, which Poland seized in 1922. It said he had a wife back in Vilna named Frume Rubinson. She had to be Bubbie Fruma, my mother's grandmother who died the year before I was born.

I still wasn't sure. These were common names and it could have been a coincidence. I needed the dry fleece on the dew-covered threshing floor before I would be convinced. Then, a key detail appeared. On the manifest, a column noted the final destination of each passenger. Most only listed a brother, father, or cousin. Nechemja-Jakob Rubinson put down the name and address of "Congregation Bnei Shalom" on the West Side of Chicago. Seeing this, I burst into tears. This was the synagogue where he had been a rabbi.

The lady from the counter was still sitting next to me and she said, "I guess you found someone you've been looking for for a long time."

She was wrong. Nechemja Rubinson was never lost. I was crying because I suddenly realized what this meant. I was looking at a fulfillment of a prophecy in the Book of Isaiah in my own life.

In the 56th chapter of Isaiah, the prophet speaks about the sons of the foreigners who join themselves to the God of Israel. It says that if they *love His name* and keep His covenant, God will bring them to his rebuilt Temple. Then in verse 7, it says God's house will be called "a house of prayer for all nations." Most people stop reading the prophecy here, but it continues in verse 8 and that is what I suddenly had clarity about as I'd never had before. In verse 8, it says:

> Thus says Lord Yehovah, He who gathers in the dispersed of Israel; I will gather others unto those I have gathered.[1]

For two thousand years, my ancestors wandered the globe, yearning to return to the Land of Israel. Every year at the end of the Passover Seder, after recounting the Exodus from Egypt, they would pray, "Next year in Jerusalem." I thought about how blessed I am that I live in Jerusalem and can walk proudly through the streets speaking the language of the prophets in a free and sovereign Jewish state. This was not some cosmic accident. I was one of those "dispersed of Israel" whom God gathered out of the Exile, giving me the opportunity my great-grandfather never had: to return to our ancestral homeland after two thousand years.

What I realized when looking at that ship's manifest is: the only reason I am alive today to enjoy this blessing is because of God's

---

[1] Isaiah 56:8.

grace. He looked at my great-grandfather with a sparkle in His eye and out of His love and compassion gathered him out of Lithuania. His name on that manifest was the difference between life and death. If he hadn't boarded the S.S. Mauretania and come over to the U.S. in 1923, he would probably be lying in a mass grave in Lithuania. The Jews who stayed behind were rounded up by the Nazis and taken out to the Ponary Forest where they were lined up and shot. Because of His immense grace, God gathered my great-grandfather out of that living hell.

What all of this means is that I can no longer *believe* Isaiah chapter 56. I believe the entire rest of the Hebrew Bible, but not this prophecy. I believe that God created the world in six days and rested on the seventh. This is a belief. I don't know it for a fact, because I wasn't there. I believe God took my ancestors out of Egypt and spoke directly to every man, woman, and child at Mount Sinai. This is a belief, but I don't know it for a fact because I wasn't there. I don't need to believe Isaiah 56 anymore. I know for a fact it's true because it was fulfilled in my life, not in some fuzzy, symbolic way but literally. God literally gathered me out of the Diaspora and returned me to the land He promised my forefathers.

As I was looking at my great-grandfather's name in the ship's manifest, I thought about Keith. His ancestors also came over to America on a ship, but I don't think I would find their names on any passenger manifest. I might find them listed as cargo. Many of my Jewish brothers and sisters are uncomfortable that I study Scripture with Keith. Some tell me I should have nothing to do with Christians because their beliefs are different. Others tell me it's fine to have a relationship with a Methodist as long as my goal is to convert him to my own faith. I never followed this advice. Instead, Keith and I decided to focus on what we have in common, while respecting what makes us distinct. We actually had an agreement that I wouldn't try to convert him and he wouldn't try to convert me.

Realizing that Isaiah chapter 56 was literally fulfilled in my own life confirmed that I made the right decision with Keith. In verse 8 of that prophecy, God calls Himself "He who gathers in the dispersed of Israel" and then promises, "I will gather others unto those I have gathered." Looking at that ship's manifest, I realized that God "gathered" Keith to where he is in his own walk of faith just as He "gathered" my great-grandfather out of the killing fields of Lithuania. I don't need to convert Keith because God is the one who gathers those who love His name; God is the one who returns His children in repentance; God is the one whose paternal instinct kicks in causing tears to well up in His eyes when He looks at us with love and compassion. I believe the words of the Psalmist who prayed:

> Turn to me and have *chen* towards me, as You always do *to those who love Your name.*[1]

I believe God has grace for all those who love His name, whether the Jew gathered in from the ends of the earth or the son of the Gentile who joins himself to Yehovah. Through His incredible *chen*, God will bring each of us along on our own journey as much as we are willing to walk with Him. It is not my job to judge others or to condemn those who have a different triangle. My job is to answer the call of the prophet Micah who said:

> He has told you, man, what is good and what Yehovah requires of you, only to do justice, love righteousness, and to walk humbly with your God.[2]

Our duty is to walk humbly alongside Him and to try to have a fraction of the grace towards our fellow human beings that our heavenly Father has for us.

---

[1] Psalms 119:132 [adapted from NIV].

[2] Micah 6:8.

Chapter 13:

A Father's Smile

I am making my way through a tunnel so notoriously constricting that Israeli hikers have dubbed it the "Birth Canal." What brought me here was a verse in the Book of Micah in which the prophet says, "though I sit in the dark, Yehovah is my light."[1] I was struggling to understand this verse, which I knew in my gut held the key to the most esoteric phrase in the Priestly Blessing, the one that says, "May Yehovah shine His face towards you."[2]

God shining His face—causing it to give us light—is obviously an *idiom* or a figure of speech. But what did it mean? I consulted numerous commentaries, lexicons, and studies, which presented a myriad of theories. I decided I needed to cut through all the mess and get back to Scripture to figure it out for myself. Then I came across this verse in the Book of Micah about God being a light to the prophet who was sitting in darkness.

I knew the prophet was speaking figuratively, but it occurred to me the image he was painting might have been one he experienced in real life. The context of the prophecy was the Assyrian invasion of 701 BCE, the one that ended with Sennacherib's miraculous defeat. Micah was from a small town in the Judean lowlands called Moresheth-gath, a town that fell to the Assyrians before their army was wiped out by the angel. Today, the ruins of Micah's hometown are known as Tel Goded, the location of the famous *Birth Canal.* I had to go.

When I arrived one hot summer morning at the *Birth Canal,* I thought maybe I had made a mistake. It looked like the opening to a

---

[1] Micah 7:8.

[2] Numbers 6:25.

fox den or something a small animal might live in. It was, in fact, the entrance to an ancient "hideout network." The countryside of Israel is peppered with hundreds of these hideout networks, first hewn out of the solid rock in the time of the Judges.[1] They were deepened and expanded during millennia of foreign invasion and occupation all the way up to the time of the Bar Kochba Revolt in the 2nd Century CE. I got down on my stomach and shined a flashlight into the opening. I imagined being an Assyrian soldier in the time of Micah, seeing one of the Jewish fighters disappear into the earth. I wouldn't go after him for all the gold in Nineveh!

It took me about ten minutes to squeeze through the *Birth Canal*, which ended suddenly in a sheer drop. Only a makeshift wooden ladder led down into the darkness. I had gone through the Birth Canal headfirst, but saw there was no way to climb down the ladder unless I went feetfirst. Back out the narrow tunnel I went. Another twenty-five minutes later, my feet finally reached the top of the rickety ladder. I then carefully made my way down into what turned out to be a gargantuan subterranean chamber.

I sat down on the floor of the chamber, covered in dust and dripping sweat. Every muscle in my body ached from the effort of forcing myself through the narrow constraints of the unyielding passageway. I imagined what it would have been like in Micah's time with dozens of Jews huddling together down here as the Assyrians pillaged the city above.

When Micah prophesied about sitting in darkness, it was an image all too real for him and his audience. The prophet himself may have sat on the floor of this very chamber after squeezing through the tight entrance-tunnel. I could understand the burning desire for the light of God while sitting down in this dark cave of despair.

When it was time to leave the hideout network, something happened that shed further light on Micah's prophecy. By then I was physically spent and didn't have the energy to once again claw my way out of the *Birth Canal*. I thought of King Hezekiah's desperate prayer for divine intervention when he faced the Assyrian invaders.

---

[1] Judges 6:2; 1 Samuel 13:6.

"The babes have reached the birthstool," Hezekiah cried out to God, using another image from everyday life, "but the strength to give birth is lacking."[1]

In plain English, I was stuck and there was no going back. I was in trouble. My mind raced with terrifying images from the movie *127 Hours*, the true story of an American mountain climber forced to amputate his own arm with a dull knife to free himself from a similar predicament.[2] Then I saw the light at the end of the tunnel, and it reminded me of the next verse in Micah's prophecy, immediately after he spoke about sitting in the dark:

> I bear the indignation of Yehovah, for I have sinned against Him… He will take me out to the light that I may see His righteousness.[3]

At that moment, I asked God in my heart to give me the strength I needed to make it out of the tunnel. He answered my prayer and somehow I was able to get going again. A few minutes later, I was in the sun, coughing the muggy musk of the tunnel out of my lungs and gulping down large breaths of fresh clean air.

I now know exactly what Micah was talking about. God taking the prophet "out to the light" after he "sat in the dark" had to be an image he and his audience experienced in this tunnel or one of the numerous others like it all over Israel. In this prophecy, God's anger was likened to *darkness* and the opposite of this was His *light*. Surely, this was what the Priestly Blessing was talking about in the words "May Yehovah shine His face towards you." *God shining His face was the opposite of Him being angry.*

When I arrived back home that night, I found confirmation of this in the Book of Job. It was in a section in which Job was reminiscing about the good old days before he lost his fortune, all his children died unexpectedly, and he fell desperately ill. Back then, he was considered an important person who people admired. Some

---

[1] 2 Kings 19:3.

[2] *127 Hours*, directed by Danny Boyle, 2010.

[3] Micah 7:9.

looked up to him so much that his mere smile could change their entire outlook on life. Job bragged about this, saying:

> I would smile at those who do not believe [in themselves];
> and they could not frown at the light of my face.[1]

Job was saying that when he would smile at those who lacked confidence it made them unable to keep frowning. The light of his face gave them the self-confidence they needed and turned their despair into hope.

This verse is a great example of one of the core characteristics of ancient Hebrew writing known as "parallelism." That's when the ancient Hebrew writer says roughly the same thing twice in two parallel halves of a verse, using different wording each time. For example, the *Song of Moses* opens up:

> *Give ear*, O heavens, let me speak;
> Let the earth *hear* the words I utter![2]

To "give ear" and to "hear" are the same thing expressed differently in each of the parallel halves of the verse. Job's parallelism speaks about *smiling* in the first half of the verse and the *light of his face* in the second half. The importance of this for the Priestly Blessing is that it proves the Hebrew idiom "to shine one's face" means, "to smile." When the priests bless us with the words, "May Yehovah shine His face towards you," they are really saying, "May God smile at you." This lines up perfectly with Micah's prophecy in which God's light—His smile—is the opposite of His anger. A verse that further confirms this appears in the Book of Proverbs:

> In the light of the king's face, there is life, and that which is pleasing to Him is like a thick-cloud of latter-rain.[3]

---

[1] Job 29:24. The phrase translated "frown" literally means to "cast down," see Jeremiah 3:12. According to some commentators, "they do not believe" means they do not believe in themselves whereas others say it means they are in disbelief that Job smiled at them.

[2] Deuteronomy 32:1.

[3] Proverbs 16:14–15. Compare NJPS: "The king's *smile* means life…"

The parallelism in this verse places "the light of the king's face" alongside "that which is pleasing to Him." When a human king is pleased, he smiles at his subjects, which can mean life for them. Similarly, God smiling at us is an expression of Him being pleased, which can mean life for us.

As I thought about my own predicament in the *Birth Canal*, I realized I had experienced God smiling at me. In the moment of my despair, He gave me the confidence and strength to push on towards the light. I "reached the birthstool," as Hezekiah put it, and God gave me the strength to be born again!

One of the greatest Biblical images of God smiling at someone, giving him the strength and confidence he needed, is the story of David and Goliath. This has always been one of my favorite Biblical stories, and I have been to the site of the battlefield more times than I can count. The events come alive when I stand in the Valley of Elah, looking out into the plain where the Philistines arrayed their forces against the Israelites. The soldiers of each army lined up shoulder-to-shoulder, staring the others down. Then, Goliath, a giant Philistine warrior, walked out between the two armies and taunted the Israelites, challenging them to send a champion to face him. The Israelites were terrified of the 8-foot-tall Gittite, clad in scale armor and carrying a gigantic sword. No one dared face him except a young shepherd boy from Bethlehem armed only with a staff sling and five smooth stones.

Six months before my visit to the *Birth Canal*, I received some new insight into the story of David and Goliath. It happened when Keith came to visit me in Israel for a period of two weeks so we could prepare for a series on Christian television entitled: *Finding Common Ground in an Ancient Hebrew Prayer.*

The day after Keith arrived, our plans were shattered completely when we faced a Goliath of our own. It started with him receiving an ominous e-mail from the general manager of the television network informing him that the filming was cancelled. She wasn't only talking about the 12-part series we were scheduled to do together. He'd been asked to come back and record a total of fifty-two programs on the network that year, and everything was cancelled. She went on to say that if Keith wanted his programs to be reconsidered, his Jewish friend, Nehemia Gordon, would be required to participate in a televised debate with a Jewish convert to Christianity. When Keith informed me of this, I could not believe my ears. We had gone from a Jew and Christian walking together on common ground back to the time of the Spanish Inquisition.

In those dark centuries, the Catholic Church pressured Jews to engage in public "disputations" with their "converted peers." The movie *The Disputation* tells the story of the most infamous of these encounters, which took place in Barcelona in 1263. In this incident, the rabbinical sage Nachmanides was forced to debate *Pablo Christiani*. This Jewish convert to Christianity was notorious for convincing the French king to require the Jews in his realm to wear the hated yellow star, a practice later adopted by the Nazis. Here I was, nearly 750 years later, and the general manager of a Christian television network was giving me an ultimatum to engage in a modern-day disputation. It was surreal. I felt like she might as well have asked me to wear a yellow star to make the picture complete.

The morning after receiving the ultimatum, I returned from walking Georgia to find Keith sitting on the sofa with an astonished look on his face, the kind he gets when something spiritual happens. He told me that when he woke up he heard a voice saying, "The Book of Ezra, stopping the work."

Keith then opened his Bible to the 4th chapter of Ezra where he read about a letter sent by the enemies of Israel to the king of Persia. In the letter, they demanded that the king stop the Jews from building the Jerusalem Temple, the place where God put His name forever.[1] What makes this letter unusual is that it is one of only a handful of passages in the Hebrew Bible written in Aramaic. At the time, Aramaic was the international language—like English today—and the Book of Ezra quotes the *Aramaic Letter* word-for-word in its original language. Keith told me he understood the significance of this when he checked his e-mail a few minutes later. There was a follow-up from the manager of the Christian television network with

---

[1] 1 Kings 9:3; 2 Kings 21:7.

more details about her ultimatum. She explained that her converted Jew was challenging the validity of the Aleppo Codex and Leningrad Codex—the two most important *Hebrew* manuscripts of the *Old* Testament—claiming instead the "textual primacy" of his own *Aramaic* version of the *New* Testament. Keith had referenced these two manuscripts of the Hebrew Bible in an earlier teaching series he did on the same television network on the subject of *God's holy name.* Because of this challenge, Keith's first series was now banned from television after airing only half the episodes. A modern *Aramaic Letter* had been sent and the work of honoring God's holy name had been stopped.

When Keith and I discussed the idea of the debate, I knew the issue was not really the Hebrew texts. The Aleppo Codex and the Leningrad Codex are indisputably the most important manuscripts of the Hebrew Bible. The Aleppo Codex is considered so important that it is on display alongside the Dead Sea Scrolls in Israel's "Shrine of the Book." The Leningrad Codex, for its part, serves as the basis of the Hebrew Bible used in every seminary and university in the world. This was really a thinly veiled attempt at pressuring me into a modern-day disputation.

The medieval disputations were set up so that the Jews could never win. They were hosted and judged by devout Christian monarchs and Catholic officials who would inevitably find statements made by the Jewish disputants to be offensive and indeed blasphemous. Even if the Jewish side formally won the arguments, they would still lose. Entire Jewish communities were sometimes massacred or forcibly converted to Catholicism following a Jewish "victory." In the movie *The Disputation*, Nachmanides epitomized the Jewish concern about these forced debates when he said to King James I of Aragon:

> When the lion invites the mouse to a disputation, your majesty, the mouse, however fond he may be of arguing would do well to avoid the disputation if he can. For the

> poor mouse does not know which to fear most, losing the argument or winning it.[1]

The king tried to allay the rabbi's fears by granting him complete freedom of speech, a novel concept at the time, along with a guarantee of protection for the entire Jewish community. When Pablo Christiani suffered a crushing defeat, he simply lied about what happened, misrepresenting the Jewish arguments in written pamphlets and tracts disseminated throughout Spain. Nachmanides countered by publishing tracts of his own that revealed the truth about what transpired. Unfortunately, this played directly into the hands of the Catholic Church, which promptly sentenced the rabbi to death. The king had given Nachmanides freedom to speak, not to write. It was only through a last-minute intervention by King James I that the rabbi's sentence was commuted to life-long exile from Spain.

When I was called out to a modern-day disputation, the thought of an anti-Semitic backlash came to mind, but I was too excited about besting my opponent. He was impugning manuscripts that form the basis of the Hebrew Bible. I was brought back down to earth when someone reminded me that beating my opponent in a debate would only make Christians hate Jews. I might get to show off my knowledge but this wouldn't be about knowledge. I knew she was right. By definition, I couldn't win. Even my "victory" would lead to hatred. This really was Barcelona all over again.

When I finally made the decision to opt out of this latter-day disputation—a choice denied Nachmanides—I was secretly relieved. I don't feel it is my calling to convince Christians to abandon their beliefs or to accept mine. I have found that one's core beliefs are a matter of personal faith and relationship with God, not something that yields to hostile argumentation.

Years ago, I saw a good friend of mine dedicate a significant portion of his time and energies to Jewish apologetics. When he passed away, it was expected of me to follow in his footsteps as a counter-missionary but my heart was never in it. The more time I

---

[1] *The Disputation*, directed by Geoffrey Sax, 1986.

spent interacting with Christians, the more I found I had in common with them. It seemed to me to be a colossal waste of time and energy arguing, when there was so much we could learn from one another. I realized you can always find differences to divide people if you want. God knows there are plenty of differences between other Jews and me and even between other Karaites and me. I decided I would focus my energies on what I have in common with people rather than on our differences.

After turning down the ultimatum, Keith and I found ourselves sitting on my couch in Jerusalem with two weeks ahead of us and no plan or direction. He had come to prepare for a television series that was now canceled, and we had no idea what to do next.

Keith was heartbroken that the series he already recorded was banned from television right before he revealed the key information to the audience. He had spent six episodes building a foundation with information on ancient Hebrew and the importance of God's holy name. When he was about to reveal the Hebrew manuscripts that recorded the pronunciation of the name with full consonants and vowels as "Yehovah," the series was suddenly banned.

"You know *Pablo* is taunting us," Keith turned to me and said.

I thought it was hilarious that Keith was referring to the people challenging us to a modern-day disputation as "Pablo," a snide reference to Pablo Christiani who orchestrated the Barcelona Disputation.

"'Pablo' is afraid the people will hear the truth about God's name," Keith continued. He explained that the "Pablo" we were facing was like the Philistine giant Goliath, wielding the power of an entire television satellite network, taunting us to come out and fight.

Comparing our situation to David and Goliath seemed a little melodramatic to me until Keith read me something this modern-day "Pablo" published on the internet. It was a vicious attack against us personally, but that wasn't what bothered me. What got me was when this modern-day "Pablo" cursed the name of the God of Israel. He took the holy name Yehovah recorded in the Aleppo Codex and Leningrad Codex and turned it into a curse. This "Pablo" claimed that Yehovah really meant "destruction," tying it to the Hebrew noun "Hovah."

After my initial horror, I thought about something that happened years earlier that made me laugh. It was back when I was a teenager at my first summer job. I had messed up causing all kinds of havoc and my supervisor took me aside for a scolding.

"Do you know what assume means?" he shouted at me.

I thought it was a rhetorical question until he provided his own answer.

"It means you make an *ass* of *you* and *me*!"

He was dead serious. All these years later it still made me giggle. How ridiculous! "Pablo" was saying something equally ridiculous, that Yehovah was derived from the Hebrew word *Hovah* meaning "destruction." It showed a complete ignorance of the most basic rules of Hebrew grammar.

Ridiculous or not, "Pablo" was cursing the name of the God of Israel and this was no laughing matter. Keith certainly wasn't laughing. He pulled a Bible off my bookshelf and started to read the story of David and Goliath in a solemn tone. When he reached the part where David went out to fight the giant, he slowed down and read one word at a time, pausing after each word. My eyes got wide, because I knew exactly what he was getting at. Most English translations render this part:

> And the Philistine cursed David by his [=Goliath's] gods.[1]

However, the Hebrew could also be translated:

> And the Philistine cursed David by his [=David's] God.[2]

This latter translation made more sense to me. Why would Goliath curse David in the name of his pagan deities who meant nothing to David? Cursing the name of David's God, in contrast, would be the ultimate offense. There could be no greater insult to an Israelite. It also explained what David did next. He took his sling and launched a

---

[1] 1 Samuel 17:43 [KJV].

[2] 1 Samuel 17:43. This is the interpretation of *Leviticus Rabbah* 17:3, which adds that Goliath was thereafter stricken with leprosy for cursing God's holy name.

stone into Goliath's head. This was the perfect response to Goliath cursing David by his God. The Torah mandates that a person who curses the name of God be executed by stoning, and David was meting out the appropriate punishment.[1] David's words before slaying the Philistine confirm his understanding of the curse:

> And David said to the Philistine, "You come to me with sword, spear, and javelin and I come to you in the name of Yehovah of Hosts, the God of the armies of Israel, who you have defied."[2]

The last word in this verse, usually translated "defied," literally means, "to taunt, to insult." David was saying that he was going to fight Goliath in the name of the very same God that the Philistine had taunted and insulted.

I realized Keith and I really were facing a Philistine giant, one that was taunting us and cursing the name of our God. I knew what we needed to do next. I told Keith to load his stuff into the car for a quick excursion out into the Judean lowlands. We were off to the battlefield in the Valley of Elah where David faced *his* giant.

Whenever I visit the Valley of Elah, I usually go to the tourist spot where most people say David collected his five smooth stones. It is conveniently located near the main road. Keith and I started out there, but then I suggested we hike up to the top of the hill dominating the northern side of the valley. I had been doing some research and discovered a recent excavation by Israeli archaeologists of an Israelite fortress from the period of King Saul. The archaeologists dubbed it the "Fortress of Elah," and I was sure it was important for locating the exact spot where David collected his stones.

As Keith and I made our way towards the fortress, I explained to him its significance. The Bible says that the Israelites faced the Philistines for forty days down in the Valley of Elah. At night, the two armies retired to hilltop fortresses on opposite sides of the

---

[1] Leviticus 24:16.

[2] 1 Samuel 17:45.

valley. We know the Philistines were garrisoned at the ancient town of Socoh to the south of the valley and the Israelites took refuge somewhere atop the hill we were climbing on the northern side. The location of the Philistine camp was never really in doubt. The Israelite encampment, on the other hand, remained a mystery until a few years ago when the Fortress of Elah was discovered.

We spent about an hour looking for the excavated remains of the Israelite fortress. When we finally found it, I was excited because I could see across the valley to the ruins of Socoh where the Philistines had camped. The real battlefield had to be in the almond orchard directly between Socoh and the Fortress of Elah, about one mile east of the traditional tourist site. The shape of the Israelite fortress was an almost perfect circle, which explained a mysterious detail in the Biblical account. Before going down into the valley to join the Israelite battle-array, it says David "came to the trench."[1] The Hebrew word translated as "trench" actually means "circle." David must have stopped off at the circular hilltop Fortress of Elah before heading down to the battlefield in the valley below.

When we were done exploring the Fortress of Elah, we marched down into the valley along the same dirt trail that David probably took on his way to fight Goliath. We then had to cross a small, dry brook to get to the battlefield. It says in the Bible that David bent down "and he chose for himself five smooth stones from the brook."[2] The seasonal brook we were crossing had to be the exact spot where David got his stones.

As Keith and I collected smooth stones of our own—the perfect souvenirs—it got me thinking about why David chose five stones when he only used one to knock Goliath off his feet. It suddenly hit me: David must have thought he might miss four times before finally hitting his intended mark.[3] I don't think this shows a lack of faith on David's part. Going out into battle without adequate ammunition

---

[1] 1 Samuel 17:20 [KJV].

[2] 1 Samuel 17:40 [NKJV].

[3] Another popular explanation is that David took the extra stones to slay Goliath's four kinsmen who were also giants (2 Samuel 21:15–22). According to 1 Chronicles 20:5 one of these giants was Goliath's brother. A scribal error in 2 Samuel 21:19 (Tav instead of Chet) caused this brother to be confused with Goliath himself.

would have been arrogant and stupid. It would have been testing the Almighty, contrary to what we are commanded in the Book of Deuteronomy, "You shall not test Yehovah your God."[1]

David knew his responsibility was to do the best he could to accomplish the job with God's help. He tried using Saul's armor and sword but had no experience fighting with them. He had spent his entire youth practicing with his sling. On two separate occasions, he even used it to deadly effect against a lion and a bear that had come among his flock. David was convinced that defeating Goliath would be no different than slaying the lion and the bear with his trusty sling.

While David knew his sling was tried and true, he also knew he could not be victorious without God's help. This was a lesson he learned from the Israelites who hundreds of years earlier conquered the Land of Israel under Joshua. Speaking about this conquest, the Psalmist says:

> For they did not inherit the land with their swords, and their arms did not save them, but Your right-hand and Your arm, *the light of Your face*, because You were pleased with them.[2]

The Psalmist is saying that the weapons of the Israelites alone did not bring them victory. It was the light of God's face—His smile—that gave them the strength and confidence they needed to achieve success. Of course, the Israelites had to do their part, going out to battle and swinging their swords, but without God's smile, their weapons would have been useless. David understood the moral of the story: he had to trust in God to smile at him, giving him the skill and confidence he needed to defeat Goliath.

Some people think they can be completely passive and expect God to bless them. David's decision to collect five smooth stones shows that Yehovah shining His face at us is about being in a sort of a partnership with God. We have to do our part—to train with our sling and collect the necessary ammunition—praying for God's smile. However, if we don't make an effort, we should not expect success.

---

[1] Deuteronomy 6:16.

[2] Psalms 44:3[4].

There is a famous parable about a man whose house is being flooded by the Mississippi River. As the waters rise, a truck drives by to evacuate him. The man refuses to get on the truck.

"I'm waiting for God to perform a miracle," he explains to the confused truck driver.

A few hours later, the rising waters force the man to take refuge on the second floor of his house. When a small boat shows up out of nowhere and invites the man to board, he replies, "No, I'm waiting for my miracle."

After several more hours, the man is grasping onto the last shingles of his roof when a helicopter drops a rope ladder down to him and begs him to get on.

"I'm a believer," the man shouts up to the helicopter pilot, "God is going to save me!"

Those are the man's last words before he drowns. The next thing he knows, he is standing before God feeling angry and betrayed.

"Why didn't You save me! Where was my miracle?" the man demands of his Creator.

"I sent you a truck, a boat, and a helicopter!" God replies, "What more did you want?"

Sometimes in life, we don't always understand the significance of God smiling on us. When the bear and the lion attacked David's flocks, he must have thought he was the unluckiest shepherd in Judah. Years later when he faced Goliath, he understood this was God preparing him for the day of battle, training him to use the weapon he would need to slay the Philistine bully. God performed the Priestly Blessing in David's life, shining His face on him. This gave him the skill and confidence he needed to be victorious.

The day after Keith and I returned from the Valley of Elah, he asked me an off-the-cuff question that turned out to be ingenious. We were back at my apartment and Keith was handling some of his precious stones, collected from the very spot where David picked up the stones he used against Goliath.

"Where do you think these stones came from?" Keith asked.

I explained that the dry brook where we got the stones was part of a natural drainage system that gets flooded with water when it rains up in the Judean Mountains. The small stones washed down into the valley from somewhere up in those mountains. They received their distinctive shape when the raging current sent them crashing into one another, smoothing out their rough edges.

"Yes," Keith continued, "but where in the Judean Mountains did these stones originate?"

I was a little annoyed by the question but popped open my laptop and turned on *Google Earth* to find the answer. It took me about fifteen minutes of staring at the screen, following tiny lines and contours to trace the Valley of Elah back to its source. I sat there gaping at the computer screen in disbelief. It turned out the stones David used to fight Goliath were washed down into the Valley of Elah from a tranquil little Jewish town in the Judean Mountains called Migdal Oz—"Strong Tower." This was the same Migdal Oz I had come across when looking for the Valley of Blessing. The stones David used to slay Goliath washed down from Migdal Oz, through the Valley of Blessing, and into the seasonal brook that runs through the Valley of Elah.

When Keith heard this, he leapt off the couch and started orating in his raspy preacher's voice to an imaginary crowd somewhere in the back of my living room, "David used the stone that came from Migdal Oz, from the strong tower of Yehovah's holy name," Keith sermonized. "He told the giant, 'I come to you in the name of Yehovah who you have taunted' and then stoned him with the smooth stone from Migdal Oz!"

I could see our trip to the Valley of Elah gave Keith the confidence he needed to face our giant, but I realized he was still lacking some ammunition. He needed five smooth stones of his own. I pulled out my cell phone and dialed one of the foremost experts in the world on the Hebrew text of the Bible. I told him I had a Methodist pastor visiting from the United States who needed to speak to him about the validity of the Masoretic Text—the Hebrew version of the Bible preserved by Jewish scribes and the basis of all modern translations.

We were scheduled to meet the professor the following week at the Hebrew University. On our way to the meeting, I took Keith for a surprise detour to the library.

"We are here for our third witness," I told Keith.

Years earlier, I had discovered the name of God written with full consonants and vowels in the Aleppo Codex and Leningrad Codex, the two most important manuscripts of the Hebrew Bible. It never occurred to me to look in a third manuscript. Now that "Pablo" was taunting us by challenging the validity of these two sources, it was time for a third witness.

We sat down at a table with a copy of the *Cairo Codex of the Prophets*—the oldest dated manuscript of the Masoretic text of the Bible. It was photographed in 1971 and published in a two-volume, limited edition. I gave Keith one volume and started skimming the other, looking for the name of God with the full vowels. After a few minutes, Keith found one possible example, but I insisted we keep looking. The photographs of the Cairo Codex were not great, and I told Keith we needed to be 100% certain. Ten minutes later, we found a second example but again, due to the quality of the photographs, there was still room for doubt. Back we went to scrutinizing the two volumes of grainy photographs.

About fifteen minutes later, I finally found it, a clear definitive example of Yehovah with full consonants and vowels. I stopped what I was doing and leaned in close to Keith, "I want to show you something," I whispered, "but this is a university library and no matter what, *you must not shout*."

Keith's mouth dropped open when I showed him the verse in Ezekiel that said:

> ...and you shall know that I am Yehovah.[1]

The "O" in Yehovah, the "missing vowel," was unmistakable. We now had our third witness.

After looking at the Cairo Codex of the Prophets, we headed over to meet the professor. He greeted us outside his office and led

---

[1] Ezekiel 7:4.

us down a dark hall to a small conference room. Keith sat down at a long wooden table opposite the professor with his hands placed palms-down in front of him. He calmly began to explain how "Pablo" was taunting us, claiming that the Aleppo Codex and Leningrad Codex were not reliable texts of the Hebrew Bible.

Keith looked the professor straight in the eyes and said in a hushed voice, "I need five smooth stones." He then flashed a raised palm at the professor with his fingers spread out to signal the number five.

The professor leaned back in his chair, raised his right index finger, and said in his thick Israeli accent, "Stone number one." This started what turned out to be a rather lengthy dissertation.

"The Aleppo Codex is the most precise Bible that was ever written," the professor announced as he launched into his first point. He explained how the Dead Sea Scrolls were physically older than the Aleppo Codex by a thousand years, but no two scrolls were identical. The Aleppo Codex preserved what ancient Jews believed to be the official version of the Bible whereas the Dead Sea Scrolls contained all kinds of minor variants from this golden standard.

For point number two, the professor got very technical, explaining about the "Masoretic notes." Keith peeked at me out of the corner of his eye, trying desperately to fight back a huge smile. We had studied the Masoretic notes together, and he knew they consisted of tens of thousands of marginal notes in ancient Jewish manuscripts of the Bible. Scribes used these notes to proofread the Bible and ensure that it was copied exactly, down to the smallest detail. The professor pulled out a piece of paper and showed Keith how many Hebrew words could be spelled in multiple ways without changing the meaning. The Masoretic notes fixed the text of Scripture down to the exact spelling of each word in each verse. This was important because some ancient Jews saw esoteric meaning in the choice of one spelling over another.

Next, the professor dropped what Keith calls a "money ball." In the lottery, a money ball is the extra ball that will double your winnings if you hit that number. The professor's money ball was a surprise even to me.

"It looks as if an angel wrote it, not a human being," the professor said in an authoritative tone.

Wrinkles spread across Keith's forehead as he turned to me and whispered, "Did he just say that?"

I was more surprised than Keith was. This professor was not speaking as a man of faith but as a scientist. Yet he said the Aleppo Codex was so accurate, "It looks as if an angel wrote it."

Keith demanded an explanation. The professor went on to tell us that when he checks most Jewish manuscripts against the Masoretic proofreading notes, he finds they match about 95% of the time. In contrast, the Aleppo Codex matches the proofreading notes 100% of the time.

"If we use other manuscripts," the professor said, "we have to compare many manuscripts to make sure the scribe didn't make a mistake, but you can trust the Aleppo Codex. The scribe didn't make a mistake. It's hard to believe a human wrote it."

"There it is!" Keith blurted out.

He was ready to go. We had only reached the second point, and he didn't need to hear anymore. But the professor wasn't done.

Point three was that the Aleppo Codex was copied by a Karaite Jew named Aaron Ben Asher who was active in Tiberias at the beginning of the 10th Century. The Karaites of that period considered every jot and tittle, every small dot and dash in the text, to be sacred revelation going back to the prophets. This is why Ben Asher spent many years proofreading this one manuscript, ensuring that nothing was lost or changed. The professor explained that Judaism was sharply divided at the time between Karaites and Rabbanites. According to the professor, the fact that both Karaites and Rabbanites accepted the Aleppo Codex proves it preserved what all Jews believed to be the authoritative text of Scripture.

Point four was that Rambam, also known as Maimonides, the great 12th Century rabbinical sage, affirmed the Aleppo Codex as the authoritative text of Scripture. Rambam was especially opposed to Karaite Jews, so his affirmation of a manuscript written by a Karaite scribe further confirms its importance.

Point five was about the missing parts of the Aleppo Codex. About a third of the codex disappeared when Arabs ransacked the ancient synagogue of Aleppo during the anti-Jewish riots of 1947. Today scholars fill in the missing portions by systematically comparing fifty Masoretic manuscripts. The most important of these is the Leningrad Codex, copied by a Rabbanite scribe named Samuel Ben Jacob.

When the professor made this last point, Keith excitedly muttered, "Money ball!"

This was significant to Keith because the Leningrad Codex was the other manuscript that preserved the full vowels of the name as "Yehovah." The fact that a Karaite scribe copied the Aleppo and a Rabbanite scribe copied the Leningrad removed the possibility of this being a *sectarian* pronunciation. Scribes from both sides knew the true pronunciation of the name to be Yehovah.

Keith was laughing with joy as the professor finished his monologue. These were the five smooth stones he was looking for. He wanted to go home and celebrate, but I had one more question. I thought I knew the answer, but wanted Keith to hear it from the professor.

"What about the validity of the vowels in the Aleppo Codex and the Leningrad Codex?" I asked.

"Pablo" was claiming the Jewish scribes arbitrarily added vowels to Scripture, plucking them out of their own imagination. I knew this wasn't true from my study of ancient rabbinical texts. One text in particular described a debate at the end of the 1st Century CE concerning the beginning of the Hebrew month. The controversy began when two witnesses appeared before Gamaliel II claiming they saw the new moon on a certain day. Rabbi Joshua overheard their testimony and knew they were lying but Gamaliel affirmed their sighting anyway.

Rabbi Joshua decided he could not observe the upcoming fast of Yom Kippur based on what he believed to be false testimony. He felt compelled to fast at home with his family one day after all the other Jews. When word of this got out, Gamaliel was enraged. In his view, the veracity of the witnesses was irrelevant. It came down to a question of authority; as head of the Sanhedrin, he alone held the authority.

The crisis was settled by Rabbi Akiva who proposed changing the vowels in a single word in Leviticus at the beginning of the section on the Biblical feasts. The original reading of the verse said:

> These are the appointed times of the LORD… you shall proclaim them (*otam*)…[1]

The key word was *otam*, "them," referring to the appointed times Israel was commanded to proclaim. Rabbi Akiva proposed changing the vowels to read the word as *atem* meaning "yourselves." According to this new reading, the verse would say:

> These are the appointed times of the LORD… you shall proclaim yourselves (*atem*)…[2]

Rabbi Akiva's new vowels placed the emphasis on those who proclaim the feasts. He concluded that even if those who proclaim the feasts—Gamaliel's Sanhedrin—are "mistaken, intentionally wrong, or deceived," their proclamation is still binding since his new reading of the verse emphasized "you …yourselves."[3]

Original reading	אֹתָם	*otam*	"them"
Akiva's reading	אַתֶּם	*atem*	"yourselves"

This change in the vowels of a single word in Leviticus became central to rabbinical theology, giving the rabbis divine authority not only over the calendar but also over other matters of religious observance. The thing is that no one reads the verse according to Rabbi Akiva's *changed vowels*. In every synagogue in the world, they still read the verse with the *original vowels*.

The discrepancy between the way the verse is read and the way it is interpreted by the rabbis has led many people over the centuries to challenge rabbinical authority. It seems to me that if the rabbis could

---

[1] Leviticus 23:4.

[2] *Mishnah*, Rosh Hashanah 2:9.

[3] *Babylonian Talmud*, Rosh Hashanah 25a interpreting Leviticus 23:2, 4, 37.

have permanently changed the vowels, they would have. The fact that they didn't, proves the vowels were already fixed at the end of the 1st Century CE. The rabbis could propose a change in the vowels for purposes of interpretation but did not have the ability to change how the vowels were actually read in the synagogue.

When I asked about the validity of the vowels in the Aleppo Codex and Leningrad Codex, the professor approached it from a different direction.

"They didn't put in vowels arbitrarily," the professor declared, "but [transcribed them] according to the received oral tradition through the scribes."

He told us he could prove this through dozens of examples where the exact same word appeared in two different verses with the same meaning but different vowels. I could see this statement perplexed Keith so I asked the professor for an example. He scribbled four Hebrew letters on a sheet of paper and asked me how to read them. They were not the four letters of God's holy name. They were *bet-resh-kuf-tav.*

"Bareket!" I announced with confidence.

He told me to turn to Exodus to the verse, which lists the twelve gems on the breastplate of the high priest. When I saw that the third gem in the list was *bareket*, "carbuncle," a large grin spread across my face.

"Not so fast!" the professor blurted out. He then told Keith to turn his Bible to Ezekiel, to a verse that contained another list of gems.

This verse had the same four Hebrew letters but Keith read them as *barkat*, also meaning "carbuncle."

My grin turned to a frown as I looked over Keith's shoulder and saw that was in fact what it said.

Bareket and *barkat* have the same exact meaning, so why the difference?

"The scribes were being loyal to a received pronunciation tradition," the professor concluded, "otherwise they would have simplified the vowels."

The professor explained that the "simpler" vowels would have been *bareket* as found in Exodus. Most Jews were familiar with this pronunciation because they heard Exodus read publicly in the synagogue on a regular basis. However, the section in Ezekiel with *barkat* was something only scholars would be familiar with. The natural thing would have been to adapt the reading in Ezekiel to the familiar reading in Exodus.

This was such a powerful example, because it recorded a subtle difference in the pronunciation of the Hebrew language between the time of Moses who wrote Exodus (*bareket*) and Ezekiel who lived nearly a thousand years later (*barkat*). This is why Rabbi Akiva could not change the vowels in Leviticus; their authority predated him by about 1,500 years.

I loved this example, because I had encountered it in real life. The mayor of Jerusalem at the time was named Nir Barkat but many people called him Nir Bareket. Until the professor explained the subtle difference between Exodus and Ezekiel, I had no idea of the ancient historical reason for the two ways of pronouncing the mayor's name.

Keith and I now had our smooth stones, the ammunition we needed to face the bully. At the end of that day, it was as if God looked down from heaven and smiled at us. Our heavenly Father gave us the confidence and the skill that we needed to face the giant.

Understanding the significance of our heavenly Father's smile illuminated an incident a friend of mine shared about his son. As a young father, he told me he came home one day to find his four-year-old standing in front of the house eating a candy bar. He was surprised because he knew the boy didn't have the money to buy candy and realized the child must have stolen it from a local shop. When the boy saw his father glaring at him, he instinctively tossed the evidence into some bushes. The father asked what he threw away, and the boy retorted, "Nothing!"

Later that night the father asked, "Did you do anything you weren't supposed to do?"

The boy admitted he was eating a candy bar he was not supposed to have. "But I didn't steal it," the boy volunteered unconvincingly, "A friend from school gave it to me."

Knowing the boy stole the candy, the father looked at his son with a scowl and said in a calm, firm tone, "If you ever want anything, just tell me."

Now, whenever the boy wants candy, he asks for it. He doesn't always get it, but his father can't help but smile, knowing his son is applying the fatherly instruction he gave him.

Our heavenly Father also gives His sons and daughters fatherly instruction when He says:

> …the word that issues from My mouth, it does not come back to Me unfulfilled, but performs what I purpose, achieves what I sent it to do.[1]

When God sees us applying what He teaches us through His word, achieving His purpose, He is pleased and looks down from heaven with a smile. This smile from our heavenly Father can give us hope when we sit in the dark cave of despair; it can fill us with confidence when facing those who taunt us; and it can imbue us with the strength to confront giants that come against us.

---

[1] Isaiah 55:10–11 [NJPS].

Chapter 14:

Back to the Mountain

He who makes peace from on high. These were the words I chanted in Hebrew as snowflakes whipped down on the white-capped mountaintop. The sign above my head read, "Summit Pike's Peak. 14,110 FT." I was there with ten strangers pronouncing a prayer in honor of my father who was being buried at that very moment thousands of miles away.

A few weeks earlier, my sister called from Seattle to tell me that my father had fallen ill and only had a short time to live. He was being treated in a nursing home in Chicago, the city where he was born and lived his entire life. My father's final wish was to spend his remaining weeks in Israel, surrounded by family. I was about to head out on a speaking tour throughout the United States and decided to fly in a few days early to help him settle his affairs. Seeing how weak he was, I knew that there was little chance he would still be alive by the time I returned to Jerusalem.

It was time to make a critical decision: would I leave my father with my sisters or cancel my speaking tour to stay with him? The focus of the tour was Keith Johnson's new book *His Hallowed Name Revealed Again.*[1] It was a follow-up to our first book together focusing on that part of the "Lord's Prayer," which says, "Hallowed be thy name." I decided that teaching people about sanctifying the name of my *heavenly Father* was a holy mission that took precedence over remaining with my *earthly father* who had my mother and four sisters to take care of him.

---

[1] Keith Johnson, *His Hallowed Name Revealed Again*, Biblical Foundations Academy 2010.

The morning I flew out of Chicago, I asked the taxi driver to stop by the nursing home for one last visit. I needed to catch a flight, so I only had a few minutes. I gave my father a hug, told him I loved him, and asked him to bless me. As he stretched out his hand, I knelt down so he could place it upon my head. He then recited the same words that he used to bless me with each Friday night, "May God make you as Ephraim and as Manasseh." This was the blessing that Jacob gave his two grandsons, the blessing of a double portion: the physical and the spiritual. My father followed this up with the Priestly Blessing in Hebrew:

> May Yehovah bless you and protect you.
> May Yehovah shine His face towards you and be gracious to you.
> May Yehovah lift His face towards you and give you peace.

When he was done, I kissed him and lumbered back to the taxi in tears. I knew this was the last time I would ever see my father.

From Chicago, I headed to Pennsylvania where I was speaking at a conference alongside Keith. Late that night, he sauntered into my room and announced matter-of-factly, "It's come-to-Jesus time, Nehemia."

"Excuse me!" I blurted out, staring at him in disbelief.

For two millennia, Christians tried to compel, convince, and otherwise coerce Jews into converting, subjecting us to cruel persecutions in the process. Keith knew that, in light of this history, the mere prospect of a conversion-talk was deeply offensive to me. When he saw that I was troubled, he snickered and quickly added that "come-to-Jesus" was a figure of speech. He meant that it was time to have a serious conversation. He launched into a soliloquy about how I had his full support if I wanted to cancel the tour and go back to Israel to be with my father in his final weeks.

When he was done, I took a deep breath and calmly told him that I did not intend to cancel the tour. My four sisters and mother were with my father in Jerusalem, and I already said my goodbyes in Chicago.

"This is not a game to me, Keith," I added pensively, "and it's not a gimmick to sell books."

We were going on the road to teach people about the name of the Father of creation, the name my Hebrew Bible recorded nearly 7,000 times, the name Keith's "Messiah" taught people to sanctify, the name that I learned to pronounce all those years ago on 9/11.

I then pulled out my Bible and opened it to the Book of Nehemiah. Keith listened as I read a passage about the Jewish exiles that held a public reading of the Torah just after returning from Babylon. When the people heard the Word of God for the first time, they began to grieve and mourn, realizing they had been sinning their entire lives. It was a feast day, a holy time, and my namesake—Nehemiah—warned them:

> Today is holy to Yehovah… do not mourn and do not cry… for today is holy to our Lord…[1]

When I finished reading the passage, I closed my Bible and looked Keith straight in the eyes.

"This opportunity to teach people about the name of our Lord is a holy time," I said to Keith, "I will mourn and cry when that time is over."

A few weeks later, Keith and I were in Albuquerque for another conference when early one morning I received a second phone call from my sister. She was at the airport boarding a plane for Israel and wanted to know when I would be joining her and the family in Jerusalem. My father was now in a coma and only had a few days to live.

"If you don't come now, you'll miss the funeral," she sternly warned me—in Israel, they bury people the same day they die.

When I told her that I was not coming, there was silence on the other end of the phone. Finally, I broke the awkwardness and said, "My calling right now is to teach people about the name of God. I believe that this will honor our father more than anything else I can do."

---

[1] Nehemiah 8:9–10.

"Oh," she finally responded in disbelief, "Ok."

She must have thought I was nuts, but I didn't care.

"Our father always taught us to stand by our convictions," I reminded her, "and I am honoring him by doing this more than I would by being at his side right now."

She knew that our father was unconventional. He didn't care what anyone thought if he believed he had the truth on his side and in that sense I am a chip off the old block.

A story that illustrates this more than anything was the Sukkah (ritual booth) that he built for our family one year. At the time, we lived in a condominium and he asked the management for permission to build a Sukkah in his designated parking spot for the upcoming Feast of Booths. When they denied his request, he was disappointed but didn't give up.

Several weeks later, my father submitted a seemingly unrelated request, to park a U-haul trailer in his parking space. Naturally, his second request was approved and he made sure to get it in writing.

A few days later, when he drove the utility trailer with a Sukkah built on the back into his parking space, the management was livid. Rather than be deterred, I think he actually reveled in their exasperation. He had worked the system and used it against those in power who wanted to prevent him from living by the Word of God, as he understood it. My sister may have been upset that I wasn't coming with her to Israel to be with our father, but I believe he would have been proud of me.

Later that week I was speaking at a church in Colorado Springs. When I was done with my presentation, Keith stood up to speak, and I pulled my cell phone out of my pocket to check the time. I saw that there was a text message from my sister. It was the middle of the night in Israel, and the hospital called in the family to be at my father's side.

"It won't be long now," she wrote.

I walked outside and called up my mother who was at the hospital by now. When she answered, I could hear the beeping of the pulse monitor in the background. She told me my father only had a few minutes to live, and she was going to put me on speakerphone so I could say goodbye. He was in a coma, and I don't know if he could hear me, but this is what I said:

> I love you, *Abba* (father). I'll see you in *Olam HaBa* (the world to come). *Baruch Dayan Emet.*

Baruch Dayan Emet—"Blessed is the true judge." This is what Jews say when someone dies. These were the last words I ever said to my father. I always had a strained relationship with him but at that moment, I felt a profound sadness. I think the natural impulse would have been to be upset with God. This must have been how Job felt in the Bible when a collapsing building killed his ten children. His wife urged him to curse God, but instead he responded to her, "Yehovah gives and Yehovah takes away. May the name of Yehovah be blessed."[1]

Rather than curse God, Job blessed the Creator's name in the moment of his greatest sorrow. *Baruch Dayan Emet* is in the spirit of Job, accepting our lot from the Almighty, even when we don't understand it, proclaiming Him to be true and just.

A few minutes later, my sister sent me another text message: "Dad is gone."

I took a deep breath and went back into the church. We still had work to do, teaching people about the name of God, so I decided to keep what happened from Keith until the event was over. When he was finished speaking, we each stood at the back of the room, signing books and answering questions. I only needed to maintain my composure for another sixty minutes or so.

About halfway through the book signing, I was put to the test when a man named Bill walked up to me. He was someone my grandmother from Lithuania would have called *a gantze meshugener*, "a complete lunatic." I first encountered Bill six years earlier in Spokane when he came to one of my presentations. He approached me back then about a book that he desperately wanted to give me. People are always trying to hand me stuff at events, and I simply can't carry extra things as I travel around speaking. I usually tell them if it's

---

[1] Job 1:21.

important enough, they can mail it to my post office box in Israel. When I told Bill this, he eyed me with a maniacal look and walked away. I didn't think much of it until the middle of the night when I was awoken by a ringing phone. It was Bill calling from down in the lobby of the hotel. He wanted to come up to my room to hand me the book. When I looked at the clock on the nightstand and saw that it was 3 a.m., I politely told him to leave it at reception. That was last I heard from him.

Now, six years later, here was Bill at a book signing in Colorado Springs coming at me like a bull in a china shop less than an hour after my father died. He demanded to know if I read his book—the one he left for me at the hotel reception desk six years earlier. In fact, I had read it and found it to be completely ludicrous. When I politely told him this he blurted out, "But it proves the Lunar Sabbath!"

"Oh boy!" I thought to myself. This was all I needed tonight.

Bill started to rant about how *Shabbat* was a Jewish conspiracy to deceive the world and how the original Sabbath was supposedly tied to the moon.

On any other night, I would have politely smiled and let him vent. Not tonight. I cut him off in mid-sentence and told him he was a paranoid anti-Semite who was not welcome here. I then asked him to leave with all the courtesy I could muster.

Bill responded by making threatening gestures and forcefully grabbing my arm. As I looked down at Bill's prying hand, I thought about the old rabbinical adage, "He who comes to strike you, rise up and strike him first."[1]

The rabbis derive this principle from the commandment in Exodus about a homeowner who finds a burglar breaking into his house at night. The presumption is that the burglar will lash out violently if challenged in the dark. The Torah gives the homeowner the right to a preemptive self-defense using deadly force.[2] Bill was obviously *meshuga*, and I didn't put anything past him.

---

[1] See *Babylonian Talmud*, Sanhedrin 72a.

[2] Exodus 22:2[1].

Then, suddenly, before I could react, a 6'7" giant that I had been talking to earlier sidled over and stood between Bill and me.

"Is there a problem here?" the giant asked, towering over Bill.

The conspiracy theorist dropped his hand from my arm and scurried out of the door without saying another word.

A short while later, I was standing outside the church waiting for Keith when two looming figures approached from the shadows. For a second, I thought maybe Bill was back to settle a score, but it turned out to be the giant and a woman he introduced as his wife.

"We want to thank you for teaching us the name of our heavenly Father," the man said in his deep gentle voice, as a tear leaked from his right eye.

Then, without warning, he and his wife grabbed me in tandem, giving me a tight hug that forced all the breath from my diaphragm. This was exactly what I needed at that moment. I had vacillated about going back to be at my father's deathbed. Now I knew I had done the right thing.

When I got back to my hotel room that night, I called my mother. It was early in the morning there, and she told me that my father would be buried that night at 8 p.m. She was broken up by his death, but there was really only one thing on her mind right now.

"Are you going to say Kaddish for your father?" she asked.

Her request left me speechless. I talked to my father years earlier about the Kaddish, a traditional Jewish prayer recited over deceased parents by their sons. This duty fell on me as my father's only son. I was always told that the purpose of Kaddish was to elevate the soul of the deceased into a higher spiritual realm. Many Jews view the Kaddish as *the* central duty that a son has towards his father. Failing to recite the Kaddish would abandon the deceased parent's soul to the nether regions of the afterlife.

When I discussed the Kaddish with my father years ago, I told him that it seemed to me to be antithetical to the basic ethos of the Hebrew Bible. The way I saw it, one of the central tenets of Scripture is that every human being is rewarded or punished for his own actions, not those of another. The prophet Ezekiel discussed this very issue when responding to the erroneous belief of the Israelites of his day that children suffer for the sins of their fathers and are rewarded for their righteousness. The common-folk expressed this in a popular proverb, "The fathers eat sour grapes and the teeth of the sons are set on edge."[1]

Ezekiel completely rejected this proverb and the beliefs that it represented. He explained that God does not judge a person for the actions of his father if he repents and does righteousness. Nor does God reward a person for his father's righteousness if he strays from the truth and turns to a life of sin. The prophet concluded:

> …the righteousness of the righteous shall be accounted to him alone…[2]

Contrary to the belief held by the common-folk of Ezekiel's day, the righteousness of the son cannot atone for the father's sins. Each person is rewarded or punished for his *own* actions. During that conversation with my father, I told him that praying for a deceased parent to ascend to a higher spiritual realm seemed to me contrary to this core Biblical concept. Now my father was dead and my mother's sole request was that I say the Kaddish prayer for him. I told her I would think about it and hung up the phone.

The next thing I did may seem rather unusual for a grieving son: I threw on a pair of swim-trunks and joined Keith for a midnight dip in the hotel hot tub. Whenever we find the opportunity, Keith and I like to take a steaming soak. We often get our best insights as our fingers and toes prune from the bubbling hot water in the early hours of the morning.

That night in the hot tub, I told Keith about my mother's request. He admitted he did not remember what the Kaddish was, although it sounded familiar to him. I reminded him that we had looked at it when researching the Hebrew origins of the "Lord's Prayer." I began to recite the Kaddish as best I could from memory to remind him, translating as I went:

---

[1] Ezekiel 18:2.

[2] Ezekiel 18:20 [NJPS].

> May His great name be magnified and sanctified. *Amen.* May He establish His kingdom in the world that He created according to His will, in your lifetimes and in the lives of the entire House of Israel, speedily and soon, and say, *Amen.* May His great name be blessed forever and ever, may His holy name be blessed, glorified, celebrated, extolled, exalted, honored, revered, and praised. *It is blessed.* May His great peace from heaven and life be upon us and upon all Israel, and say, *Amen.* He who makes peace from on high, may He make peace for us and for all Israel, and say, *Amen.*

When I was finished, Keith had a look of shock on his face.

"You're kidding!" he blurted out.

I was so used to what the Kaddish represented to me that I hadn't stopped to think about the actual words of the prayer. I lowered myself up to my neck in the hot bubbling water and thought about what I had just translated.

The Kaddish opens by praising God's holy name, speaks about God's will as the dominant force in the Universe that He created, and calls for the establishment of His Messianic kingdom on earth. After some more praising of the Creator's name, it ends with the future hope of world peace. This was almost precisely the message Keith and I had been traveling around preaching; the same message contained in what Christians refer to as the "Lord's Prayer." It was a message with a solid foundation in the Hebrew Bible and hence *common ground* for Jew and Christian alike. Then again, I was always taught the purpose was to raise a loved one's soul into a higher spiritual plane, which to my mind made it a base superstition. So I still wasn't convinced about the validity of reciting the Kaddish for my father.

After more soaking in the hot tub, I headed back to our hotel room where I did a quick internet search on the history of the Kaddish. I found out the belief about improving the lot of a deceased parent's soul was a late innovation in Judaism. The prayer was originally recited by Torah scholars at the end of their sermons, based on the verse in Ezekiel that said:

> And I will be magnified, and I will be sanctified, and I will be known in the eyes of many nations and they will know that I am Yehovah.[1]

The idea was to end Bible sermons with a charge to go out into the world and sanctify God's holy name. As I was reading this, Keith was in his bed snoring, and I had to stifle a shout of excitement.

I took a deep breath and went back to reading. I learned that the next stage in the development of the Kaddish was to recite it when a Bible scholar died. This was done at the end of the traditional seven days of mourning, when the eldest son gave a Bible sermon of his own to continue his father's legacy. The son would end his Bible sermon by reciting the Kaddish prayer, just as his father had done during his lifetime.

"How appropriate," I thought.

My father was a rabbi, a learned scholar, and I was continuing his legacy through my writing and lectures. Rather than say the Kaddish as a rote ritual, I decided I would do it in the spirit of those earlier generations who sanctified the name of God as a way of continuing the legacy of their fathers. By now, it was 2 a.m. and I needed to get some sleep. I would decide in the morning where and when to say the prayer.

When I woke up five hours later, Keith was already packing his bags. We weren't scheduled to fly out of Colorado Springs until late that night but he wanted to get an early start. We were only thirty minutes from the base of a mountain where Keith had a life-changing spiritual experience ten years earlier. He had wanted to take me to *his* mountain—Pike's Peak in Colorado, ever since I took him to *my* mountain—Mount Sinai in Egypt.

Keith's desire to visit Mount Sinai was spurred on by the mystical experience that I had atop that mountain a couple of years earlier when God took away my pain. I ended up going there a second time, with Keith, a few weeks after Egyptian dictator Hosni Mubarak was ousted from power in a popular uprising that came to

---

[1] Ezekiel 38:23 (so according to Metsudat David, taking the *hitpael* verbs as passive).

be known as the "Arab Spring." It was a surreal time. Law and order had broken down in Egypt and the consensus was that it was a dangerous place to visit. I remember telling my mother that Keith and I were heading down to Eilat, Israel's southernmost city.

"Don't go near the Egyptian border!" she warned hysterically.

Little did she know that we were heading straight for the border. When we got to passport control on the Egyptian side it was as if we had walked into a ghost town. We were the only tourists there and the passport agent had snuck off for a nap. One of the guards had to go wake him up so that we could get the necessary stamps to enter the country. From the Egyptian border, we took a taxi down to Nuweiba and from there to the mountain where we arrived shortly after midnight.

The first time that I went to Mount Sinai, I came there under a great burden of emotional pain. The second time, I was in immense physical pain following a neck injury. When I first talked with Keith about accompanying him, I was in so much agony that I couldn't even sit up in a chair for more than thirty minutes at a time. I told Keith that I would only undertake the journey if he agreed to carry my backpack. From experience, I knew that the Bedouin who ran Mount Sinai charged a hefty fee for water. My backpack was loaded with several large bottles that I brought with me from Israel. When Keith strapped my unwieldy bag onto his back, he started to whine like a little girl. It was after midnight. He was exhausted from traveling all day. He didn't realize the bag would be so heavy. *Kvetch, kvetch, kvetch.* I told him it was only a three-hour hike up the mountain.

"Or you could rent a camel," I said condescendingly.

Before I knew it, Keith was mounting a camel.

"See you at the top," he said laughing, as the contemptuous beast carried him into the night.

Caving in, I also rented a camel. The camel-driver caught up with Keith and tied the reins of his camel to the back of mine. Now, my camel was walking through the murky night with Keith's camel in tow.

"My camel is yoked to yours," Keith shouted from out of the darkness. "This is a picture of our relationship. You lead and I follow," he continued.

"Just wait and see," I squawked back.

As our camels lumbered up the precipitous trail, they kept shifting positions. Sometimes mine would be in front, with Keith's following. At other times, Keith's camel would take the lead with mine in faithful pursuit. At still other times, our camels would walk side by side.

"Now this is a true picture of our relationship!" I announced contently.

It only took two hours for our camels to reach the Bedouin shelter just below the peak. I had been there two years earlier in the autumn, but now it was winter and much colder. We decided to get some rest in the cave-like shelter before heading to the summit. We stretched out on some old mattresses and fell fast asleep.

When we awoke a few hours later, it was sixty minutes before sunrise. We hurried up the steps and found only a handful of people at the peak. We each went off to different corners and prayed while we waited for the sun to make its first appearance. About fifteen minutes later, we met at the highest point of the mountain and watched the sun burst forth from behind the mountains.

On my first visit to Sinai, God caught me off guard, blind-siding me with a mystical experience. This time, the Litvak in me was on high alert, ready to repel any spiritual incursion. I had decided there was no way I was going to have a second God-experience. But I guess God had different plans. As I stood at the highest peak of the mountain bathing in the warm rays of the rising sun, I suddenly felt a fatherly love overwhelm me, crashing against my soul like waves on a rocky shore, sending me into deep convulsions of sobbing. I don't know if it lasted ten seconds or ten minutes. Then in my mind's eye I saw God reach down from heaven, place his hand upon my shoulder and say, "I still love you my son."

Through my wailing I croaked, "Todah, Abba. Thank you, Father."

I felt a great solace overcome me. It had been two years since I stood in this very spot and even after all this time my heavenly Father's love had not wavered.

Now six months later, Keith and I were on a train heading up to the top of Pike's Peak in Colorado. My father's funeral was about to start on the other side of the world. I had experienced God's fatherly love at the top of a mountain on two different occasions and it occurred to me that a mountaintop was the ideal place to say the Kaddish prayer. I told Keith about my plan and he was excited.

"But I need ten people," I added hesitantly.

Keith asked what I was talking about.

I explained that the prayer was about sanctifying the name of God in the moment of your greatest sorrow, the way Job did when his children died. Tradition mandated that this be done in a public forum with ten people responding "Amen," the Hebrew word for "truth."

"I will answer amen to your father's prayer," Keith announced, "but I don't know where you'll find another nine people."

After an hour of painstakingly crawling up the mountain, the train finally arrived at Pike's Peak. It was four degrees below zero and snowing, so everyone bolted from the train straight into the cafeteria and gift-shop. The mass of tourists bustled around buying trinkets, hot chocolate, and fudge. They carefully avoided the frigid summit they had come to see, only fifty feet outside the rear entrance of the visitor's center.

"I want to do this at the summit," I shouted in Keith's ear over the din of busy travelers.

Keith nodded his head and looked nervously at his watch. The conductor had told us that we needed to be back aboard the train for the descent down the mountain at precisely 11:20. "What do you call someone who arrives at 11:21?" the conductor asked over the loudspeaker on the way up the mountain. "A hiker!" he quickly responded to his own question.

Keith nervously flashed ten fingers at me twice. He was reminding me that the train would be leaving in twenty minutes. I didn't have much time to convince ten strangers to come out with me into the freezing snow and participate in a memorial prayer for a man they didn't know. I decided to start at the end of the cafeteria and work my way through, one table at a time.

"My father died last night," I announced to the folks at the first table. "They are burying him right now in Israel, and I need ten people to come outside to say a traditional Jewish prayer with me. It's a prayer that sanctifies the name of God. Would you come outside and help me say the prayer for my father?"

"It's too cold," the skinny, middle-aged woman responded in a thick German accent. She started to spout some excuse about her mother having the sniffles, but I didn't have time, so I walked over to the next table and repeated my speech.

The man at the second table looked at me sympathetically and announced that he was a Christian pastor. He asked if he could pray for me.

"Yes, please," I snapped back.

The man put his hand on my shoulder, leaned his head down, and recited a short prayer for God to comfort me.

"Now will you come outside with me to say the prayer for my father?" I asked matter-of-factly.

The man nodded his consent and his wife and another couple with whom they were traveling joined.

Five down, five more to go.

Ten minutes later, I was outside with Keith and ten strangers. I explained to them that all they needed to do was answer "Amen" whenever they heard me say it. I looked around at my *minyan*, the quorum of ten that I needed for the prayer. They weren't exactly *kosher* in the traditional sense. Not one of them was Jewish and they included both men and women—-rabbinical law requires ten Jewish males. Nevertheless, to me this motley crew coming together to console a Jew, who just lost his earthly father by sanctifying the name of our heavenly Father, was a picture of Biblical prophecy. It was a living expression of the words of Zechariah:

> …ten men from nations of every tongue will take hold—
> they will take hold of every Jew by a corner of his cloak and

say, "Let us go with you, for we have heard that God is with you."[1]

It was also a picture of the verse in Ezekiel that served as the inspiration for the Kaddish, the verse in which God proclaimed, "I will be known in the eyes of many nations and they will know that I am Yehovah."

I may not have been fulfilling the *letter* of tradition, but I felt like I was acting in accord with the *spirit* of what my father taught me. One of my first memories of my father was sitting on his right knee in our family living room every Sabbath afternoon. He would drill me on this rabbinical teaching he had about *Avram Avinu*—our forefather Abraham.

"Nehemia Shalom,"—he always used my middle name *Shalom*, meaning *Peace*. "Nehemia Shalom," he would ask me in his deep bass voice, "how old was Avram Avinu when he came to know his Creator?"

I would squeak out the formulaic answer that he taught me, "The Rambam says he was forty and the Ra'avad says he was three."

I must have been three years old myself and probably didn't know who Abraham was. I certainly had no idea that Rambam—Maimonides—was the preeminent rabbi of the Middle Ages and that Ra'avad was his chief critic. This was the first Scripture that my father ever taught me—at least that I can remember—and looking back on it now, I realize that it contained a profound lesson.

I think most people hearing a man teach his preschooler about a disagreement of Biblical interpretation between a pair of 12th Century rabbinical philosophers would think that the father was confusing his son.

"Just give him the answer," they might say.

But my father taught me something far more important than the answer. He taught me with my very first words of Torah that it is okay for people to have different opinions, even about something as important as the Bible. He truly *blessed* me in the literal sense of the

[1] Zechariah 8:23 [NJPS].

Hebrew word for blessing by placing me on his *knee* and teaching me to respect those who share a common love for the Creator of the Universe, even if they have different interpretations, doctrines, and creeds. My quorum may not have been kosher in the traditional sense, but I was fully convinced it honored the blessing that my father bestowed upon me.

The time finally came for me to recite the Kaddish before my ad hoc *minyan*. It was more difficult than I thought it would be. My whole life I was taught this is what you say when your parent dies. Now I was saying these words and all of a sudden it was real. My father was dead. The prayer was only seventy-six words long, but they were the most difficult words I have ever uttered in my life. I had to struggle to force each syllable out of my mouth through a gauntlet of sobs and hailstorm of emotion. At the end of each line of the prayer, the ten strangers responded through the piercing, stinging snow in a chorus of "Amen."

I finally got to the Hebrew formula ending the prayer, "He who makes peace from on high, may He make peace for us and all Israel, and say, Amen."

The sentiment of Job, of sanctifying God's name in the moment of my greatest sorrow, was now more than a mere platitude. It was something I experienced. I felt a wave of peace pass over me. I was still sad but saying the prayer, sanctifying the name of the Creator of the Universe, comforted me.

On the long ride down the mountain, I sank into deep thought about the Jerusalem Municipal Cemetery where my father was now interred. The last time I set eyes on that cemetery was the day I went to see Israel's memorial to the victims of 9/11, located in a forest two miles west of the city. It was the tenth anniversary of that vicious attack and ten years to the day since I learned how to call on the name of the living God. Only five Israelis were killed the day the towers came crashing down, but the memorial paid tribute to *all* of the victims, listing their names on a series of large bronze plaques.

Names are so important in Hebrew culture that it is considered a curse for someone's name to be forgotten. In contrast, it is considered a blessing to *remember* a name by *mentioning* it.[1] I decided to *remember* the victims by *mentioning*—reading out—some of their nearly 3,000 names. Kerene Gordon. Dominique Pandolfo. Daniel C. Lewin. Jennifer Lynn Kane. Brett T. Bailey. Thierry Saada. "*Yehi zichram baruch,*" I concluded—*may their memory be blessed.*

When I had finished reading out the names, I walked over to a small garden behind the memorial that looked out across the Arazim Valley in the direction of the Jerusalem Municipal Cemetery. The names of the victims still echoed in my head and it got me thinking about God's holy name, a name that was now virtually forgotten around the world. In contrast, the name those nineteen men shouted when they committed those horrific acts of murder was better known today than the eternal name of the Father of creation. At that moment, I felt an overwhelming conviction to offer a prayer with the holy name of God, the very same name He instructed the priests to proclaim over the people when blessing them. Then it occurred to me what I really needed to do was offer a prayer in the spirit of that blessing, the Priestly Blessing, the blessing from our Father. I closed my eyes, leaned my head down into my hands, and prayed:

> Oh Yehovah, let Your name be known from the east all the way unto the west, from the rising of the sun all the way unto the place of its setting. For You are the one who blesses us and protects us, You are the one who smiles at us with a twinkle in His eye, You are the one who looks at us performing miracles overtly and covertly. You, Yehovah, are the one who gives us peace. May we have personal peace in our lives today and may all mankind soon in our days stand shoulder to shoulder calling on Your name in a time of global peace. Amen.

---

[1] Exodus 17:14; Deuteronomy 9:14; 25:6, 19; 29:20[19]; Psalms 9:5[6]; 109:13.